United States
Department of
Agriculture

Forest Service

**Southern
Research Station**

General Technical
Report SRS–154

The Work of the Civilian Conservation Corps: Pioneering Conservation in Louisiana

James P. Barnett and Anna C. Burns

Authors:

James P. Barnett, retired Chief Silviculturist and Emeritus
Scientist, Southern Research Station, U.S. Department of
Agriculture, Forest Service, Pineville, LA; **Anna C. Burns**, retired
Library Director, Louisiana State University, Alexandria, LA.

Civilian Conservation Corps, 1933-1942

Cover

Civilian Conservation Corps (CCC) enrollees of Camp F-8 weeding and thinning pine seedlings
in a nursery bed at the U.S. Forest Service, Stuart Nursery near Pollock, LA. With the help of
CCC enrollees, the Southern Forest Experiment Station planted almost 750,000 seedlings in
experimental studies on the Palustris Experimental Forest southwest of Alexandria, LA. This
research effort provided much of the information used to develop guidelines needed to reforest
the South.

Photo credits

The photographs are primarily from the files of the U.S. Department of Agriculture Forest
Service; annual reports of the Civilian Conservation Corps, District E, Fourth Corps Area,
U.S. Army; the Louisiana Department of Agriculture and Forestry; the Natural Resource
Conservation Service of the U.S. Department of Agriculture; and the Southern Forest Heritage
Museum and Research Center. Other sources are identified where possible.

May 2012

The Work of the Civilian Conservation Corps: Pioneering Conservation in Louisiana

James P. Barnett and Anna C. Burns

ABSTRACT

The Civilian Conservation Corps (CCC) was a public work relief program that operated from 1933 to 1942 in the United States for unemployed, unmarried men from relief families, ages 18-25. A part of the New Deal of U.S. President Franklin D. Roosevelt, it provided unskilled manual labor jobs related to the conservation and development of natural resources on the Nation's forest and agricultural lands. The CCC was designed to provide employment for young men in relief families who had difficulty finding jobs during the Great Depression while at the same time implementing a general natural resource conservation program in every State and territory. Men enrolled in the CCC planted over 2 billion trees, built over 125,000 miles of roads and trails, constructed over 6 million erosion control structures, and spent 6 million workdays fighting forest fires. (No women were ever enrolled in the CCC.) Their efforts pioneered methodologies for conserving and restoring forest and agricultural lands. An equally remarkable accomplishment was the program's effect on the lives of the CCC young men, changing despondent youths to confident, well-prepared men who would capably defend the United States during World War II.

Keywords: Civilian Conservation Corps, forestry, New Deal administration, reforestation of southern pines, soil and water conservation.

Contents

Preface

The Civilian Conservation Corps (CCC) was created in 1933 by U.S. President Franklin D. Roosevelt in response to the Nation's dire unemployment and imperiled natural resources. The CCC had a great impact on Louisiana by employing youth to work on conservation projects throughout the State. Although the influence and accomplishments of the CCC have been recognized widely, there is little specific information on enrollees and camps in Louisiana.

This book is the result of a cooperative effort I undertook with Anna Burns, wife of Edmond Burns, Forest Management Chief of the Louisiana Forestry Commission (now Louisiana Department of Agriculture and Forestry). Anna Burns began years ago to collect oral histories of CCC enrollees, facilitate annual meetings of enrollees, and document information about Louisiana CCC programs, and in 2009, donated her collection of CCC documents and materials to the Southern Forest Heritage Museum and Research Center (SFHM) at Long Leaf, LA. Although the SFHM cataloged and stored the materials in the Dr. Anna C. Burns CCC Collection, it has not had the resources to pursue further development and use of the collection, hence this document.

Our research reveals a program that spurred large-scale development of forestry and conservation across the country, and in Louisiana, and that provided an unprecedented but realistic opportunity for improving employment, developing the economy, and restoring an environment long damaged by neglect.

James Barnett
Pineville, LA

Introduction

Franklin D. Roosevelt took office as president of the United States in 1933 in the midst of the Great Depression. By this time, the economic "crash" that had started on October 24, 1929, (commonly known as Black Thursday) had led to an 89 percent decline in the stock market. Complicating matters was the severe drought that had begun to turn the country's midsection into what came to be known as the Dust Bowl. The country's jobless rate had reached over 25 percent, and children and youth were particularly affected by the Nation's new level of poverty, with nearly 50 percent of children without adequate food, shelter, and medical care. Roosevelt, facing these crises, ran for president on his New Deal platform, promising to get people back to work.

U.S. President Franklin D. Roosevelt developed the Civilian Conservation Corps program both to provide employment and protect our environment.

On March 21, 1933, just a few days after his inauguration, Roosevelt proposed establishment of the Civilian Conservation Corps (CCC) "to be used in simple work, not interfering with normal employment, and confining itself to forestry, the prevention of soil erosion, flood control and similar projects." Ten days later, Congress enacted legislation approving the measure, and it was signed into law on April 4, 1933. A few days later, CCC camps began to be established.

Although Roosevelt had a clear mandate for the program, he was not without opposition. Senator Huey P. Long, who had political control of Louisiana and presidential aspirations of his own, broke with Roosevelt over patronage issues of the CCC program and attacked the act on the floor of the U.S. Senate, calling it the "sapling bill" and declaring that Louisiana did not want any of Roosevelt's trees planted on its land and that he would "eat every one of them that comes up in my state" (Humphreys 1964a). After Long was assassinated in the State capitol in Baton Rouge, LA, on September 10, 1935, his populist colleagues remained in leadership positions within the State. The success of the early camps, however, overwhelmed any such opposition. Most towns began to lobby for camps in their communities, and when established camps were moved or closed, there was an outcry of opposition.

Senator Huey P. Long opposed the establishment of the Civilian Conservation Corps because of his own national political ambitions

Robert Y. Stuart, as Chief of the Forest Service, did much to support development of reforestation capability. The Forest Service nursery at the Pollock Civilian Conservation Corps camp was named in his honor.

Frequently called Roosevelt's Tree Army, the CCC has been called the most successful of the New Deal programs. With stated goals of employing young men and curtailing the destruction of America's natural resources, the CCC enrolled unmarried men between the ages of 18 and 25, and whose families were on public or private relief rolls. Early on, the program was proposed for use only on public lands.

During Congressional deliberations, Major Robert Y. Stuart, Chief of the Forest Service, U.S. Department of Agriculture, asked that State and private land be made eligible as work areas. Otherwise, men from the East would have to be transported west of the Rocky Mountains, where 95 percent of the public land lay (Salmond 1967). Although soil erosion control work was allowed on State and Federal land, it was restricted on private land to activities already authorized by other laws. The future of CCC work in soil conservation on private land was largely delayed until April 1935 when the Soil Conservation Act was signed. The newly renamed Soil Conservation Service (SCS) took over soil erosion camps previously under the general administration of the Soil Erosion Service (SES) and significantly increased the work in soil and water conservation (Helms 1965).

Another change in the program was expanding enrollment to include veterans of World War I, a change that came a year after the "Bonus Army march" of 1932, when 17,000 World War I veterans and their families protested in Washington, DC, demanding immediate cash-payment of their service certificates. The marchers were protesting the decision by the U.S. Congress to delay payment on the veterans' service certificates until 1945 (there were no other benefits for veterans then). To help alleviate concerns of veterans, Roosevelt issued an executive order allowing the enrollment of 25,000 veterans in the CCC while exempting them from CCC requirements that applicants be unmarried and under the age of 25. In 1934, two CCC camps of veteran enrollees began their establishment in Louisiana, and others were added during the program. In 1936, Congress passed the Adjusted Compensation Payment Act, authorizing immediate payments to the veterans (Daniels 1971).

Administration of the Program

The U.S. Army was responsible for administering the Civilian Conservation Corps (CCC). Louisiana CCC companies were established within District E of the Fourth Corps Area of the U.S. Army, which included Louisiana and the southwestern portion of Mississippi. Headquarters for District E of the CCC was located at Camp Beauregard near Pineville, LA. On April 21, 1933, headquarters and supply companies were established for the camps. On April 29, 1933, the U.S. Army's Fourth Corps headquarters in Atlanta authorized the establishment of four forestry camps in District E.

Initially, enrollees were transported to Fort Barrancas near Pensacola, FL, for processing, shots, and physical conditioning prior to being transferred to camps where they would serve out their enlistments. Later this process was carried out in Camp Beauregard. Normally, enrollees spent 2 or 3 weeks in these conditioning or "boot" camps.

The U.S. Departments of War, Agriculture, the Interior, and Labor had primary responsibilities for activities of the program and their level of coordination was remarkable. The selection of individuals for enrollment was the responsibility of the Department of Labor. The War Department's responsibilities included physical conditioning, transportation, camp construction and administration, and supplies. The Department of Agriculture was responsible for planning and conducting work projects on National forests in the contiguous United States as well as Alaska and Puerto Rico, and on certain private lands within those States. The Department of the Interior had similar responsibilities on lands under its jurisdiction, including all State, county, and local park lands (Salmond 1967). Employees from these sponsoring agencies, called "user agencies," supervised work projects assigned to the CCC companies.

All recruitment was conducted at the State level through an agency and quota designated by the Department of Labor. To be eligible for enrollment, a CCC recruit had to be a U.S. citizen, in sound physical shape, unemployed,

Major Gooding Packard was an early district commander of District E Civilian Conservation Corps. He was highly respected, and a camp was named in his honor.

unmarried, and between 18 and 25 years old. Moreover, a recruit had to demonstrate his financial need. The program did not grant enrollment to women.

Recruits initially enrolled for 6 months. In return, each CCC recruit received food, clothing, shelter, medical care, and an allowance of $30 per month. Recruits were required to send an allotment of at least $25 a month to a dependent. In late September 1933, the Department of Labor announced that reenrollment was possible so that a CCC recruit could work a combined total service period of 2 years.

The program prohibited discrimination based on color, race, creed, or politics. Even so, African-Americans and other ethnic minorities encountered difficulties in accessing the program. In 1933, African-American camps were segregated from White (Caucasian) camps, and true integration was rarely enforced.

Nationally, the Forest Service sponsored the majority of CCC camps, but the U.S. Army was assigned responsibility "for all matters incident to command of units," including construction, supply administration, sanitation, medical care, hospitalization, and welfare. At the time, the army was judged the only organization capable of this massive undertaking. The Forest Service or other sponsoring agency was responsible for actual work projects, technical training and execution, and supervision of work forces (Salmond 1967).

Number and Type of Louisiana Camps

The Forest Service, U.S. Department of Agriculture, sponsored the greatest number of Civilian Conservation Corps (CCC) camps nationally, due in part to the recently completed Copeland Report that documented Forest Service needs (Wakeley and Barnett 2011). But in Louisiana, little land—Federal or State—was available for CCC projects. The first camps were established on Kisatchie National Forest land, but only eight were installed on that land through the duration of the program. Only four State parks were created, and one camp was established on the Alexander State Forest near Woodworth. Most CCC camps were established on private land. Under the auspices of the Forest Service, the Division of Forestry of the Louisiana Department of Conservation (later named Louisiana Forestry Commission) managed a large number of forestry camps, and the Soil Conservation Service hosted numerous camps across the State related to erosion control and soil conservation needs. Other agencies sponsored camps to work on drainage problems and to build roads along levees. The levee camps in Louisiana were the only ones in the national program. In a unique arrangement, two U.S. Army camps were established on the Barksdale Field near Shreveport, LA, and one at Jeanerette, LA, on Federal land. Many camps had a relatively short life because they either completed their assignment or were moved to meet other needs. Over the 9 years of the program, 84 camps were developed in Louisiana, with 20 to 25 camps active in any year. All camps were designated by letters and numbers indicating their classification based on land ownership or type of work. Table 1 lists these designations for camps in Louisiana.

The organization of CCC companies reflected the role of the U.S. Army. A chain of command was clear, and standard plans were developed for camp layout. Canvas tents were originally intended for all CCC camps, but the army and the American Forest Products, Inc. demonstrated the cost feasibility of lumber products. A shift to wooden structures quickly occurred with potential benefit to lumber and other local industries and with improved living conditions.

Enrollees were sent to camps in various parts of the country, according to the need for workers. In theory, the chosen camp would be fairly near the enrollee's home. Nevertheless, many individuals assigned to camps in the West were from the Eastern United States (Salmond 1967). Homesickness was a reported problem. Most enrollees had never before been far from home.

Table 1—Designations of CCC camps established in Louisiana

Camp designation	Work area and land ownership	Sponsoring agency
F	National forest	U.S Forest Service
S	State forest	Division of Forestry, Louisiana Department of Conservation
P	Private forest	Division of Forestry, Louisiana Department of Conservation
SCS	Private farm land	Soil Conservation Service
SP	State parks	National Park Service; Division of Wildlife, Louisiana Department of Conservation; State Park Commission
A	Barksdale Field and other government property	U.S. Army, New Iberia Government Experimental Farm
L	Levee roads	Louisiana State Board of Engineers
D	Drainage	Bureau of Agricultural Engineering
ASCS	Military camp	Agricultural Stabilization and Conservation Service
BF	Federal game refuge	Bureau of Fisheries and Wildlife

Barracks in a typical Louisiana Civilian Conservation Corps camp with cots and footlockers.

Basic Camp Organization and Management

A Civilian Conservation Corps (CCC) company stationed in Louisiana used the standard organizational structure for an U.S. Army infantry company of the time, which typically consisted of a complement of 200 men. Each company was normally divided into platoons of 50 men, and each platoon fell under supervision of a CCC leader or assistant leader.

Regular U.S. Army officers were in charge of each company or camp. Typically, each camp was led by a military staff of four officers: a commanding officer, an executive officer, a camp surgeon, and a mess/canteen officer. The commanding and executive officers were charged with administration of the camp, the surgeon was in charge of medical needs, and the mess/canteen officer was responsible for the operation of the camp's mess hall and canteen. The recreation and fitness programs were handled by a contract educational advisor, once these positions were created for all camps. Reserve officers from the U.S. Navy, U.S. Marines Corps, and U.S. Coast Guard also could be called to active duty to serve on CCC camp staffs when needed, although their time served with the CCC did not count in their records of military longevity.

Early in the program, noncommissioned officers (NCOs) for the program were drawn from regular military units. The NCOs functioned as first sergeant, supply sergeant, and mess sergeant, and carried out orders of the officers in day-to-day running of the company. The NCOs were soon replaced by "local experienced men" (LEMs)—nicknamed "long eared mules" by CCC workers—who were trained to handle the kinds of supervisory and administrative duties and responsibilities that NCOs normally held in the companies. The LEMs were hired, based on the recommendation of the commanding officer and project superintendent, as foremen who directly oversaw the project work conducted by the company. Up to 24 LEMs could be hired to work at each camp (Louisiana CCC Oral History Project 2011).

CCC leaders and assistant leaders could be named from the ranks of company enrollees. These individuals could provide administrative duties and function as foremen of work crews. Due to the added responsibilities of these individuals, they were paid $45 and $36 a month, respectively, with the standard $25 dollar allotment from their salaries sent home to their families.

Upon arrival at camp, enrollees were usually given two sets of blue denim work clothes and a renovated army olive drab uniform for dress purposes. Initially, the uniforms tended to be too large for the thin young enrollees, and they "had to wrap the pants around them to stay on and the boots were so large they walked right out of them" (Burns 1983). In 1938, however, Roosevelt ordered issue of a special, spruce-green dress uniform to all enrollees. The president, while visiting a camp at Warm Springs, GA, had been disagreeably surprised by the poor quality of the dress uniforms. Shoddy clothing, he believed, weakened morale, and he immediately asked the Department of the Navy to design a special CCC uniform. These were in widespread use by 1939.

The uniforms were provided at no cost to the enrollee, but he had responsibility for cleanliness of his clothes. Since the CCC crews

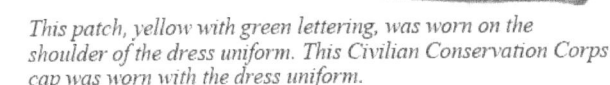

A camp office provided administrative space for the military staff.

This patch, yellow with green lettering, was worn on the shoulder of the dress uniform. This Civilian Conservation Corps cap was worn with the dress uniform.

TOP: U.S. President Franklin D. Roosevelt visits a Civilian Conservation Corps camp for lunch. At such a meeting, he decided that the quality of the Civilian Conservation Corps uniform should be improved. ABOVE: Civilian Conservation Corps enrollees were allowed to wear chevrons on their uniforms to indicate their status in the company. These were different from the regular army insignias, and the enrollee had to purchase them. The insignias were red in color with green striping.

worked hard, their work uniforms became soiled quickly. At some camps, women from the nearby community would wash clothes for a fee of 25 cents per bag. In other camps, enrollees as a business venture washed clothes for others on weekends for a small fee. Otherwise, enrollees washed their own clothes. Cleanliness was emphasized.

A typical camp site consisted of about 12 wooden buildings, which included 4 barracks with a capacity of up to 50 men each, a mess hall, and other supplemental buildings such as officers' quarters, garages, tool houses, and bath houses. Although the army officers were in charge of the camps, their jurisdiction did not extend to the work projects. These were under the project superintendent and foremen, who were assigned from the sponsoring agencies and were responsible for the CCC crews' activities for 8 hours a day, 5 days a week (Humphreys 1964b).

Spike, or side, camps were authorized to work on temporary projects located at a distance from the main camp that made daily travel to and from the camp impractical. These camps were usually under the supervision of the user agency and limited to about 25 enrollees.

Camp Routine

Camp routine was determined largely by the army—the bugle sounded at 6 a m., enrollees dressed in blue denim work clothes and reported to formation by 6:30 a.m., when they might engage in a few minutes of "sitting-up exercises" before breakfast. At 7 a.m., they "policed" the grounds, at 7:15 a m., they stood inspection, and roll call for work began at 7:45 a.m. (Humphreys 1964a).

Enrollees with experience and capability could be upgraded in position to leaders; the leaders, in turn, worked under foremen from the sponsoring agency who walked from group to group making suggestions and giving specific instructions. At noon, the men returned to the camp for lunch if the camp was near the worksite; if it was not, a truck brought the men their meals, which were eaten from army mess kits during the 30-minute lunch period. At 3:30 p.m., the men returned to camp and had assigned duties and work details that lasted to 4:30 p m. On certain days, all men engaged in brief military drill, without arms. These drills served them well as most of these men went on to serve in the military during World War II.

Between 4:30 and 5 p m., the men showered and changed into the dark green, army-type dress uniform. At 5 p.m., the men gathered in small groups for mail call and announcements. The senior leaders called the men to attention and the flag was lowered as the bugler sounded retreat (Humphreys 1965). Dinner followed, consisting of well-balanced food—meat, vegetables, dessert, and coffee or milk. Enrollees were allowed to eat as much food as they desired—the cooks were instructed to prepare food as long as the crews were hungry.

Civilian Conservation Corps (CCC) crews typically came to camps malnourished and hungry. Quantities of good food were very important for the work they were assigned. One enrollee described his situation when enrolling as constant hunger. Otis Miller came from a large family that sharecropped and he was the oldest child. The family had to live on a rabbit a day. They bartered for three or four 0.22 caliber shells at a time to hunt rabbits. A political friend promised to get him into the CCC although he had not yet turned 16 years of age. He was enrolled a few days later (Burns 2000a).

Civilian Conservation Corps crew at a worksite eating lunch from mess kits.

LEFT: *Camp kitchen staff at work preparing meals for Civilian Conservation Corps crews.* RIGHT: *Civilian Conservation Corps enrollee baking pies for camp meals.*

He describes the enrollees' diet situation:

We were about 100 pounds when we went in there. It wasn't long before we gained 15 pounds apiece. You could eat a full meal there. I'll never forget what they called 'slum-gullion'... They took bread, we referred to it light bread, but you call it bread today. The difference between bread and light bread was cornbread. We called it light bread because it was so good we thought it was cake. Out at the CC camps, they cooked tomatoes and whatnot in with the bread and made a kind of bread stew, but we called it 'slum-gullion.' You'd fill up on that and we weren't used to getting plum full, so we started gaining weight. Then of course at other meals they'd have something else and a big breakfast. It was always a good breakfast, and you'd eat until you couldn't wiggle. Everyone got rosy-faced and gained weight.

At breakfast, we had bacon, eggs, grits, milk, coffee, and fruit juice. And, they had fruit for breakfast, too. Fried eggs, you could take three eggs in one hand and break them and dump them. Three more and dump them. Put those in the frying pans and fry them. Fill it full of eggs and say, 'How many do you want, boy?' And you'd slap them on that plate. Feed them up; bacon, eggs, grits, biscuits, coffee, milk, fruit, syrup, and butter. We needed it, but like I said, we averaged about 100 pounds and some of us got out of there weighing about 130 pounds. That was in our growing stages, and it was good for us (Burns 2000a).

Evening routine varied from day to day and by camp. If the enrollee was not called out to fight fire, he was free and could go to the camp library to read, to work in a woodshop on a project, go to the recreation hall for Ping-Pong or pool, or join others in basketball or baseball. Others might get permission to ride the nightly truck run to the nearby town.

Not all men were free in the evening. Those classified as illiterate were required to attend classes and others could sign up for one or more classes per week. Lights were turned out at 10 p m. with a "bed check" at 11 p m.

The full daily schedule resulted in an emphasis on "on-the-job" training. The objective of this training was to produce efficient and intelligent workers who, when they left the ranks of the CCC, might find gainful employment elsewhere.

CCC workers were free on weekends, unless inclement weather during the week held up work that had to be made up. But normally, Saturday was devoted to activities such as sports, choral practice, movies, dances, and even running the camp newspaper. Most camps held about four dances annually, with women invited from surrounding communities and with music often furnished by camp swing bands. To the consternation of local males, CCC crews seemed to have some money in their pockets for soft drinks, popcorn, and a movie, and were considered well dressed in their uniforms. Dances, then, were frequently interrupted by forest fires set to ensure the CCC crews were called to fight fires instead of dancing with the local girls (Troll and others 2010).

But for many workers, the weekend was time for more than relaxation. For some, the weekend including dabbling in journalism with most camps contributing regular activity reports to the national CCC newspaper *Happy Days*. Most of the newspaper work was done by CCC workers as part of their course of study in journalism classes on weeknights and weekends (Salmond 1967). Many camps published their own newspapers, and by August 1935, there were 1,122 CCC camp journals; journals from Louisiana camps bore such esoteric titles as *The Spade, Zig Zag, Rocky Crest,* and *The Pirogue.*

On Sundays, religious services were held in all camps. There were full-time CCC chaplains on duty, as well as part-time contract clergymen, but unpaid clergymen from neighboring towns also served camps. The chaplains preached, counseled, visited the sick, buried the dead, and performed the few marriages between CCC workers and local women.

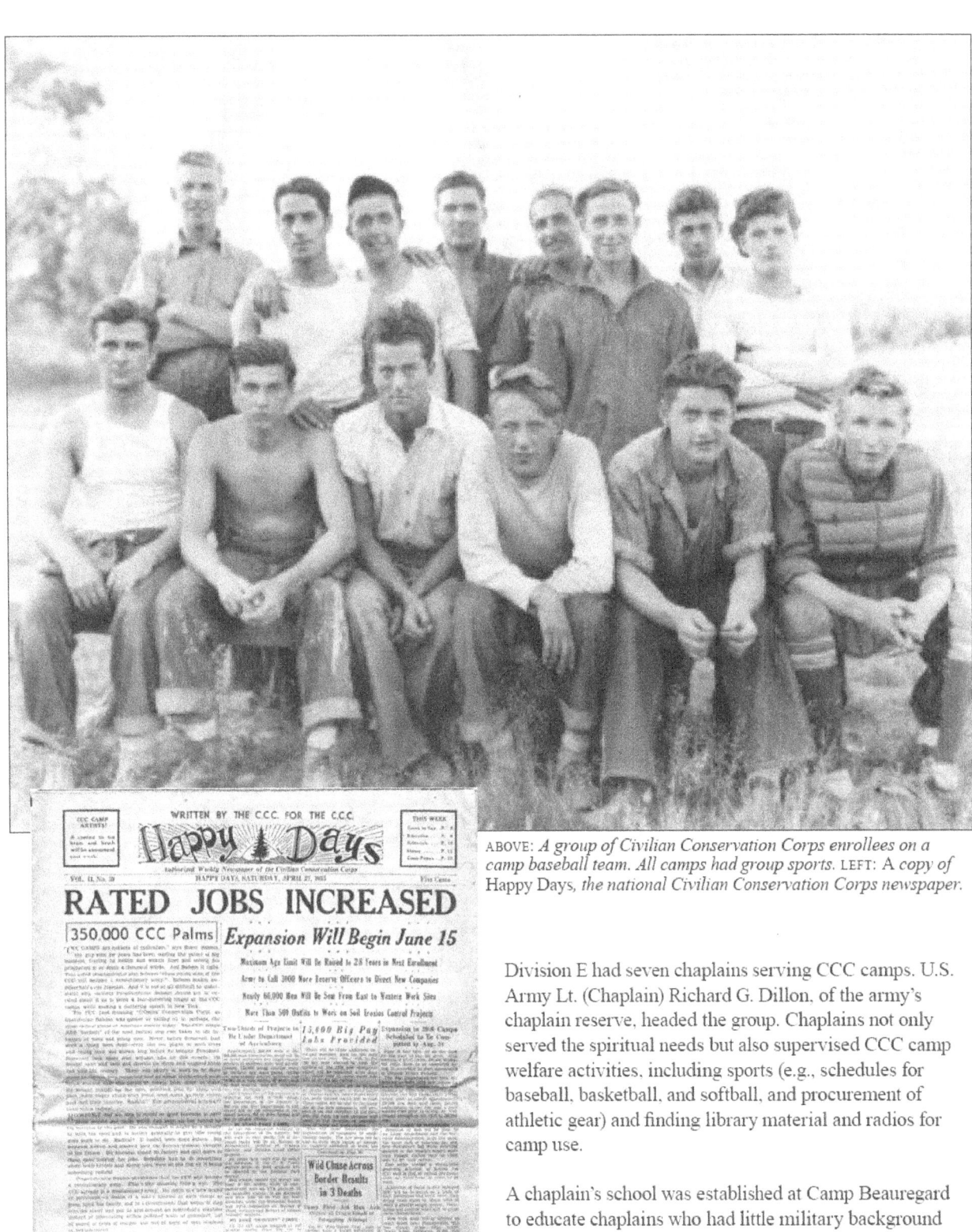

ABOVE: *A group of Civilian Conservation Corps enrollees on a camp baseball team. All camps had group sports.* LEFT: *A copy of* Happy Days, *the national Civilian Conservation Corps newspaper.*

Division E had seven chaplains serving CCC camps. U.S. Army Lt. (Chaplain) Richard G. Dillon, of the army's chaplain reserve, headed the group. Chaplains not only served the spiritual needs but also supervised CCC camp welfare activities, including sports (e.g., schedules for baseball, basketball, and softball, and procurement of athletic gear) and finding library material and radios for camp use.

A chaplain's school was established at Camp Beauregard to educate chaplains who had little military background in the organization and conduct of CCC camp life. This was an excellent opportunity for chaplains to gain military knowledge and help them relate to experiences of CCC enrollees.

Lt. Dillon left active duty with the military when his responsibility with the CCC ended; he returned to church responsibilities in Monroe. Shortly afterward, he died from an automobile accident. His death caused sorrow among

9

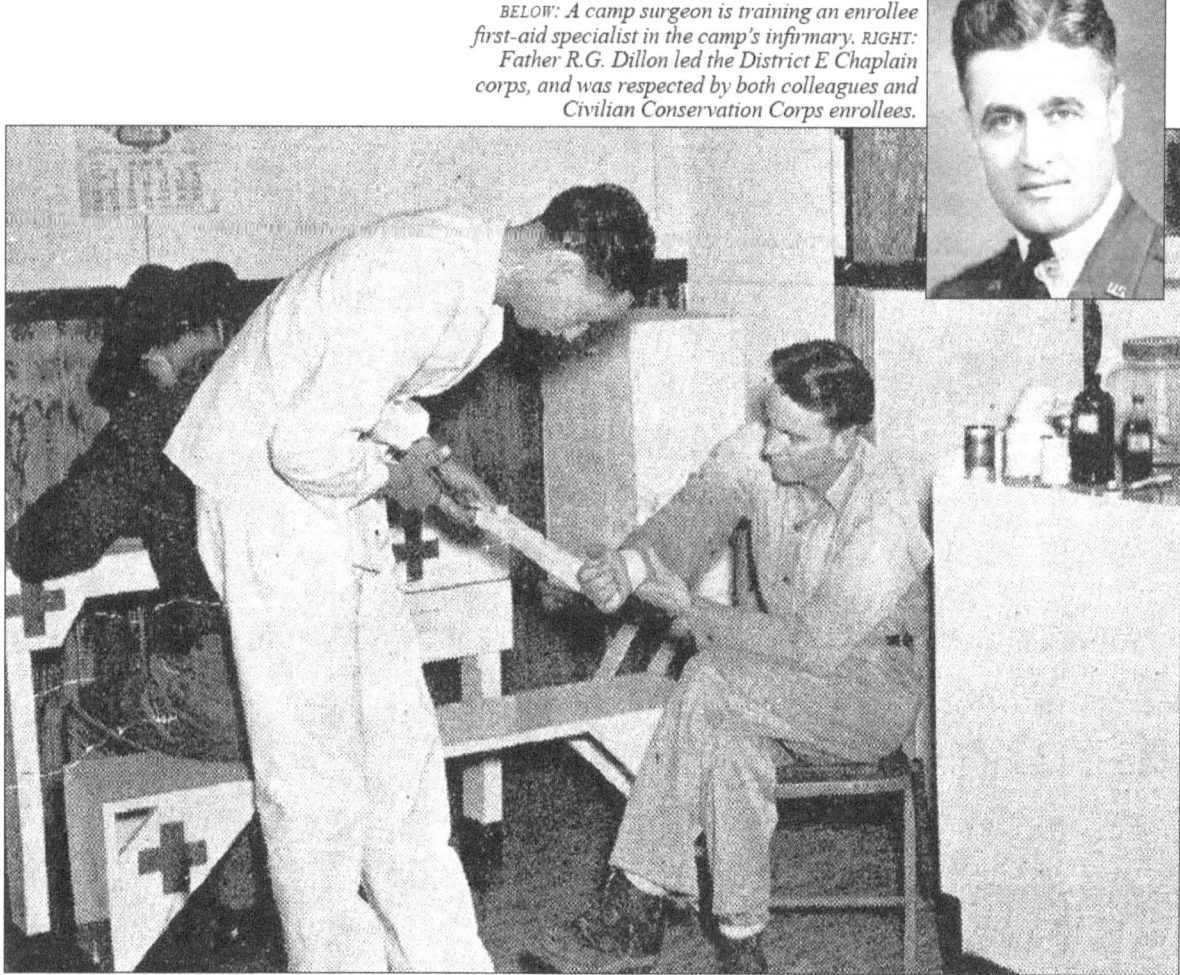

BELOW: A camp surgeon is training an enrollee first-aid specialist in the camp's infirmary. RIGHT: Father R.G. Dillon led the District E Chaplain corps, and was respected by both colleagues and Civilian Conservation Corps enrollees.

military colleagues and CCC enrollees who had grown to respect him for the positive influence he had on their lives.

Medical care was provided to all enrollees. Each camp had a camp surgeon assigned to the staff. Usually the doctors lived at one camp but also served another close-by camp. In 1939, District E had 23 reserve Army medical corps officers, two contract surgeons, and four Army dentists. Each camp had a dispensary with several beds for sickness or injuries. First-aid assistants trained from the enrollee cadre provided care until a doctor was needed (U.S. Army 1939). Camp Beauregard had an infirmary with a 50-bed capacity. For more serious cases, local hospitals were used.

CCC workers received dental care from dentists who periodically came to the camps for 2 weeks to provide routine cleaning as well as dental restoration.

Medical care of the enrollees exceeded the care available in most of the local communities. M.J. Hair, who served as a doctor in camps F-3 and S-1, described the extent of care provided to enrollees: "Each doctor traveled daily to visit the camps under his responsibility. Trained first-aid specialists handled more routine cuts or bruises. If an enrollee had a temperature above 100 degrees, he was transferred to the Camp Beauregard Infirmary or to a local hospital for treatment" (Burns and Burns 1997).

Educational Programs

The educational level of Civilian Conservation Corps (CCC) enrollees varied widely by region. Only 8 percent of the enrollees of the Fourth Corps Area had completed high school before coming to work for the CCC. In June 1933, CCC leadership, acknowledging the need for vocational training and further education of CCC enrollees, developed a plan to join with universities and extension services in helping CCC workers become "self-sufficient and useful citizens," with an emphasis on eliminating illiteracy.

Camp education advisors and assistants were appointed, and, by 1937, there were 1,100 CCC school buildings with libraries exceeding 1,500,000 volumes nationally. The CCC education program boasted instruction "at all levels, including basic literacy, elementary, high school and college courses, and vocational training" (USDA Forest Service 2011). More than 90 percent of all enrollees were participants in some facet of the educational program.

There was an emphasis on on-the-job training because of the full daily schedule of the enrollees. Training was provided in a number of fields, including auto mechanics, various types of construction work, heavy equipment maintenance and repair, drafting, surveying, and office procedures. The many kinds of technical forestry and conservation activities enabled CCC workers to find employment with the Forest Service and other agencies. The kind of training varied greatly from camp to camp (Humphreys 1964a). In Camp 255 near Dry Prong, for example, typing was the most popular course, as was a course on cooking and baking taught by a former army cook from a nearby veterans CCC Camp, and a number of CCC workers took classes in dancing and in etiquette, both as taught by the wife of the company commander.

In Company 280, a Soil Conservation Service (SCS) camp near Minden, the educational advisor developed, in cooperation with Minden service garages, an apprenticeship program in automobile mechanics for 15 men. Another apprenticeship program gave six CCC workers training in the printing trade through work at a local newspaper. Other Company 280 offerings included courses in French, art, and carpentry.

At Camp P-58 near Olla, civil engineering was a popular course taught by an engineer of the Forest Service. The class schedule consisted of an hour of lecture each week and a full afternoon a week devoted to field work, "where actual field experience in running lines and handling the compass and transit" were part of the training. The class made a detailed map of the camp, drawn to scale. This camp also acquired a library of over 300 books that came from the superintendent of schools, community donations, CCC funds, and the personal library of the educational advisor.

The emphasis at Camp F-1, near Pollock, was on vocational courses and on-the-job training through use and repair of camp machinery. There were courses in motor mechanics,

ABOVE: *Auto mechanics was one of numerous types of on-the-job training provided to enrollees.* RIGHT: *Training of the enrollees in the levee camps had a focus on providing a basic educational program.*

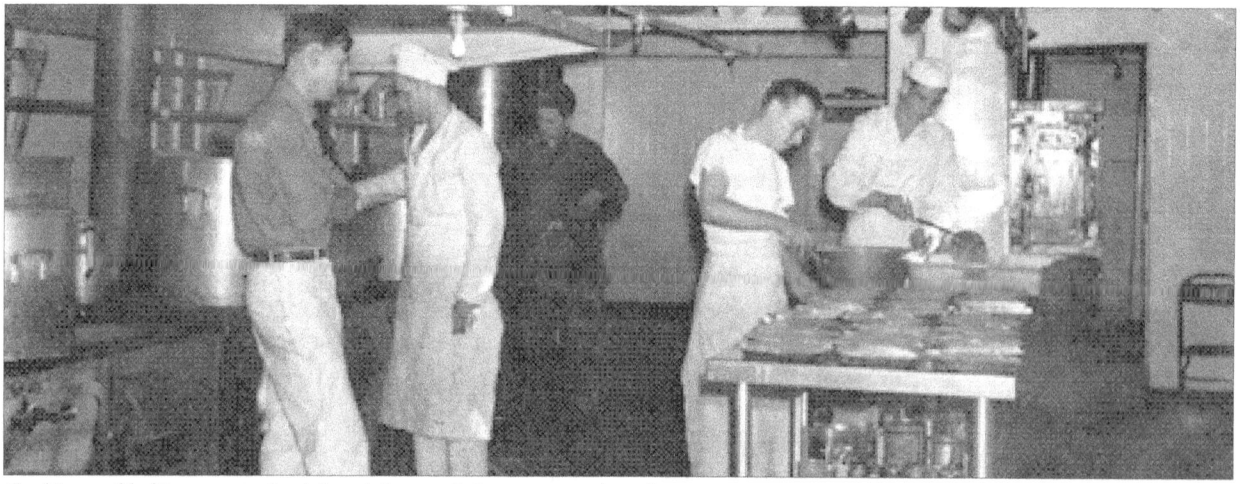
Cooking and baking was on-the-job training carried out at a number of camps.

surveying, electricity, forestry, and agriculture, including a class that produced a successful vegetable garden.

In all camps, illiterate CCC workers were required to attend classes. At the two camps with African-American enrollees in Louisiana in 1934, the greatest challenge was the elimination of illiteracy. A complete elementary school program was established with the emphasis on fundamental subjects. There was limited vocational and on-the-job training, probably because these were levee-road camps where a wide variety of work experiences was limited.

As the educational programs became organized, additional training was provided to the educational advisors, their assistants, and other CCC instructors. Special instructors came from groups such as the army, the Forest Service, the SCS, the American Red Cross, and State colleges and universities.

In camp at Arcadia (SCS-7), L.C. Ewing, the educational advisor, wrote a column called "At the Camp" almost every week for the *Bienville Democrat* to acquaint people of the community of the purpose and activities of the CCC. Columns covered the educational program, camp dances in which the community leaders were persuaded to act as chaperones, the town and camp "clean-up" campaign, and results from sports contests. Another strong feature was the publication of the camp newspaper, *The Rocky Crest*. Many instructional activities were related to the publication of this newspaper (Humphreys 1964a).

A special educational project was undertaken at the State Park Camp (SP-5) near Mandeville, LA. Fourteen CCC workers, including some from other camps, built a four-room house and most of the furniture that went into it. The men planned the project and undertook work that included

carpentry, brick work, painting, and landscaping. On completion of their project, the CCC workers held an open house for the community to demonstrate their work.

John Hunter, who later became president of Louisiana State University, was the educational advisor for Camp Vernon (F-4) near Leesville, LA, in 1939. When interviewed by Humphreys (1965), he indicated that he left his position at Camp Vernon with a feeling of frustration about his accomplishments. In retrospect, however, he realized that more was accomplished than he first thought. Hunter realized that teaching the illiterate to read and write was one of the most important accomplishments of the program, as was upgrading the education level of most enrollees. He observed, too, that the influence of the older men from the sponsoring agencies, chaplains, and community leaders positively shaped the lives of CCC workers.

Hunter also thought the camps' recreational programs, which gave many of the workers the first opportunity in their lives to participate in organized sports, was a great value to the general physical and mental health of the young men. Hunter believed that whatever weaknesses the CCC program had, it was useful during the Depression years by financially helping families in need and employing young men who had few alternative solutions to their problems in the 1930s (Humphreys 1964a).

The CCC education program had a major effect on society because a larger number of youths entered the CCC each year than entered the Nation's universities and colleges as freshmen (Oxley 1936). Over 3 million young men worked in camps and were discharged from its ranks, and 1 out of every 9 men who registered for military conscription under the country's Selective Service System had received CCC training (Gilbert 1941).

Segregation Issues

The Civilian Conservation Corps (CCC) was established under a policy of no tolerance for discrimination by color, race, creed, or politics. To assure that African-Americans and other minorities had equal access to the program, the CCC was mandated to allocate 10 percent of its enrollment to African-Americans—a quota based on the proportion that African-Americans represented on the Nation's relief rolls and not on their proportion of the Nation's population.

Early in the program, these goals were difficult to achieve. Society at the time made integration of individual camps hard to accomplish, particularly in the South. Direction of the program changed so that camps were filled with either African-American or White workers and integration became a reality only when there were not enough African-Americans to warrant establishing separate camps.

As decisions on locations of camps began, it became obvious that some communities strongly resisted forming an African-American camp in their area. A camp near Minden, LA, was moved because of this opposition. Later in the program, this resistance diminished because of the economic resources that camps brought to the area and because the military administration of camps overcame many of the social concerns. An African-American camp was later welcomed near Minden in north Louisiana.

Another problem in carrying out the nondiscrimination policy was the army's general resistance to integration of its regular military units. One indication of this attitude was how camp information was presented in annual reports that District E published of CCC activities. Information on camps with African-American enrollees was relegated to the back of the report and separated from the others by a blank sheet.

African-American enrollees benefited from the Civilian Conservation Corps as much as did White enrollees, or more.

U.S. President Franklin D. Roosevelt hoped that the program would not discriminate against African-Americans, but the president never expected that his program would overcome the country's deep-rooted racial segregation (Harper 1992).

Although racial integration of camps was a reality in some CCC camps around the country, it was not a reality in District E. In 1935, following racial disturbances in Texas and California, Robert Fechner, who headed the CCC program, curtailed recruitment of African-Americans for new camps (but allowed it to continue for openings in established African-American camps) (Harper 1992).

Salmond (1967) concluded that with 200,000 of 2.5 million enrollees being African-American; the CCC was not replete with racial discrimination, because the 10 percent national goal for African-American enrollment was almost met. Others concluded that racial discrimination in the CCC may not have been as acute as in other New Deal programs, but that it was routine (Harper 1992). Inequality existed, but most observers agreed that treatment in African-American camps was similar to that in White camps, and the benefits that accrued to African-American enrollees were positive and comparable to those of Whites (Wandall 1935, Wimbush 1972).

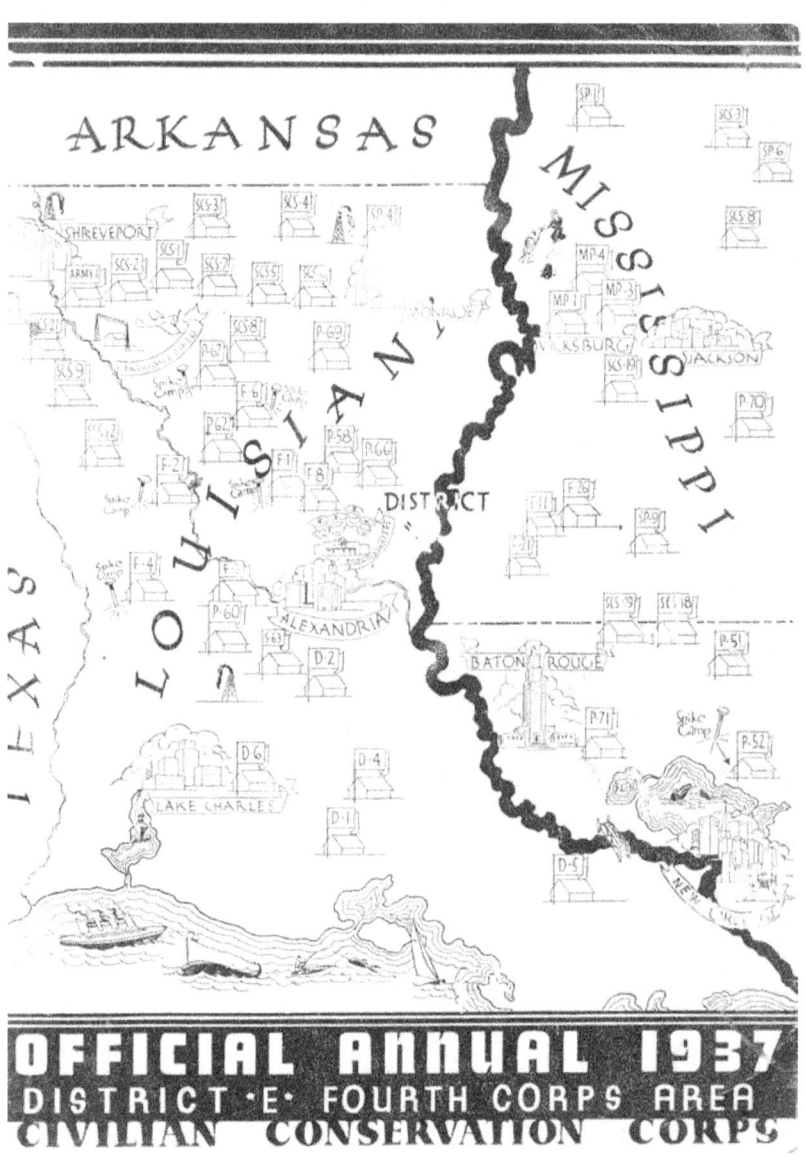

Annual reports on current camps, such as this, were prepared each year by the U.S. Army. Distribution of the reports apparently was limited, as copies today are difficult to find.

Camp Stories

While information is limited about Civilian Conservation Corps (CCC) camps, their workers, and activities, this report endeavors to present as much information as possible about Louisiana's CCC camps. The CCC had such a significant and long-term effect on the economy and development of forestry and other conservation programs that it deserves to be understood and appreciated (Burns 1983). The information in this chapter is organized by camp designation and sponsoring or "user" agency (table 1).

F—Kisatchie National Forest, Forest Service, U.S. Department of Agriculture

The first camps in Division E authorized by the U.S. Army on April 29, 1933, were forestry camps. Two camps each were established in Louisiana and Mississippi. The two in Louisiana were sponsored by the Kisatchie National Forest of the Forest Service. The camps were designated F-1 and F-2 and assigned reforestation responsibilities. Another six camps in Louisiana were sponsored by the Forest Service during the duration of the CCC program.

Philip H. Bryan was supervisor of the Kisatchie National Forest when the Civilian Conservation Corps program began.

Initially, the Forest Service camps were the only camps that had a focus on reforestation. The aggressive tree planting program required a facility for seedling production and guidelines for the producing and planting of nursery stock. The Kisatchie National Forest's Stuart Nursery was established with CCC support, and Philip C. Wakeley of the Southern Forest Experiment Station, who was developing such guidelines based on research conducted with the Great Southern Lumber Company at Bogalusa, LA (Wakeley 1935), was transferred to the nursery. Research scientists were assigned to conduct studies at the nursery, and CCC enrollees carried out many of the nursery and field outplanting efforts. The Palustris Experimental Forest was established for an outplanting site for evaluating the developing nursery practices (Barnett and others 2012). This collaboration between the CCC and the Forest Service produced research data that

became the basis for Wakeley's (1954) document "Planting the Southern Pines," which provided the basic technical knowledge to reforest the South following World War II.

Company 1476, Camp F-1 (also known as Camp Woodrow Wilson), Pollock—Named in honor of U.S. President Woodrow Wilson, this camp started up on May 23, 1933, when CCC enrollees from New Orleans were transported from their conditioning training at Fort Barrancas, FL, to Pollock, LA. After a tent camp was erected and establishment of the camp complex had begun, early work by the Camp Woodrow Wilson CCC crews entailed road and firebreak construction and maintenance, telephone line construction, firefighting, and fire presuppression activities.

CCC crews from Company 1476 began clearing land for a tree seedling nursery in September 1933. Later named the Stuart Nursery after the then late Chief of the Forest Service, Major Robert Y. Stuart, it became one of the largest pine tree nurseries in the world with the capacity of 45 million pine seedlings, but only about 25 million were grown annually. In February 1934, the CCC workers began construction on a great earthen dam near the nursery for the purpose of providing irrigation water. Water was pumped by two 235-horsepower engines over a mile to where it was conveyed into a network of 8 miles of sprinkler systems. CCC crews completed the nursery in June 1934. Buildings needed to support the nursery operation were constructed by the Works Projects Administration, including a cone and seed processing plant designed to supply the seed needs of the nursery. The Stuart Nursery complex became the largest and most modern such facility in the Nation.

The tent camp was converted into a number of wooden structures that served the needs of the company well. In 1935, a recreation hall, infirmary, and educational buildings were added to the camp.

Camp Woodrow Wilson, or Camp F-1, turned over the work of nursery operations to Camp F-8 in July 1935. The new work program for the CCC crews of Camp F-1 consisted of road and firebreak construction, planting pine seedlings in season, bridge building, firefighting, and telephone line construction and maintenance.

The CCC crews of Company 1476, during 4 years of the company's existence, built 5 steel bridges, 38 miles of roads, and 164 miles of firebreaks. They planted about 4 million

TOP LEFT: *One of two stone pylons established at the entrance to Stuart Nursery.* TOP RIGHT: *This rustic sign pointed the way to the Stuart Nursery, a major project of the Civilian Conservation Corps in Louisiana that provided hundreds of millions of pine seedlings for reforestation efforts.* BOTTOM: *Company 1476 of Camp F-1 was first organized with tents for housing. These were soon replaced with wooden barracks and other camp buildings.*

pine seedlings, built 4 lookout towers, spent 3,096 days fighting forest fires, and installed 29 miles of telephone lines, as well as constructing the Stuart Nursery and its lake that provided irrigation water. The Company 1476 CCC crews made an amazing contribution to establishing forestry practices in the State. The educational program consisted of a wide variety of vocational work. Their sports teams were very successful, winning several district championships.

During the spring of 1937, Camp F-1 provided drivers to aid in the rescue and evacuation of marooned persons in flooded areas of Louisiana. The CCC crews worked day and night moving hundreds of flooded individuals and tons of supplies to a rescue camp.

The nursery and associated lake constructed by Camp F-1 men have had a lasting effect on the reforestation of the South. Pine seedlings produced at the nursery reforested hundreds of thousands acres of cutover forest land. The Stuart Nursery was closed in 1963, but Stuart Lake continues to be a delightful area for picnicking and swimming in the summer months.

Company 1491, Camp P-57, Bastrop; and Camp F-2, Provencal—Company 1491 was organized on May 17, 1933, at Camp Beauregard, with 188 recruits from North Louisiana comprising the enrollee cadre. After a conditioning period of 3 weeks, the company was moved to a campsite 12 miles north of Bastrop, LA, where CCC crews erected buildings, laid walks, and performed other work building Camp P-57, which was dedicated on July 1, 1933 (U.S. Army 1934).

The Kiwanis Club of Bastrop, LA, had the distinction of naming the camp. Morehouse was chosen after Abram Morehouse, one of the most distinguished persons in the history of that region of the State. Camp Morehouse's assignment consisted of building roads, fire-breaks, telephone lines, and fire lookout towers as well as fighting fires. The camp was sponsored by the Division of Forestry, Louisiana Department of Conservation.

On September 20, 1935, portions of the company were released to form the Calhoun and Homer camps. Work at Camp P-57 was completed October 29, 1935, and the

TOP: These Civilian Conservation Corps workers are beginning construction of the dam to create a lake to provide irrigation water for the nursery. It was named Stuart Lake in recognition of the late Chief of the Forest Service. BOTTOM: Site of Camp F-2 was located in a wooded area near Provencal. This camp provided considerable support to Camp F-8, which operated the Stuart Nursery at Pollock.

remaining company moved by trucks to Camp F-2, located 12 miles south of Provencal on Louisiana Highway 39 in the Kisatchie National Forest.

On June 26, 1935, Company 1477, which established Camp F-2, was moved to a Pollock site where it became Camp F-8. Company 1491, then, occupied the Provencal F-2 site. After Company 1491's move to Provencal, additional buildings were added to the campsite. An outdoor amphitheater was constructed, and flowers and shrubbery were planted throughout the camp area. Camp Kisatchie was selected as the camp's name.

Under the supervision of the Forest Service at Camp F-2, CCC crews from Company 1491 planted approximately

16 million pine tree seedlings, erected 61 miles of metallic and 12 miles of grounded circuit telephone line, constructed 150 miles of travelable firebreak, built 15 and maintained 40 bridges, erected one 100-foot steel and two 50-foot wooden fire lookout towers, and put up 34 miles of range and 13 miles of plantation fencing (U.S. Army 1937, 1939). They provided fire protection for 120,000 acres of forests, and collected cones for use at the Stuart Nursery. The CCC crews who climbed trees for cone collection were called "tree monkeys" (Louisiana Oral History Project 2011).

Educational instruction was provided primarily by the using service, the Forest Service. The educational department had a staff of 13, a four-room educational building, a well-equipped woodworking shop, and a darkroom for

LEFT: A Civilian Conservation Corps worker climbs a pine tree to dislodge cones for seed collection. BELOW: This 100-foot steel lookout tower with cabin near Gardner was constructed by Civilian Conservation Corps enrollees of Camp F-3.

photography. They provided instruction in 19 subjects. In 1939, 10 enrollees took extension courses and received college credit from State Normal College (now Northwestern State University) at Natchitoches, LA.

Company 1491 had strong athletic teams. The baseball team was undefeated in 1937. A swimming pool was constructed by the enrollees during their leisure time, and was a popular summertime spot. Two examiners and 12 senior American Red Cross Life Savers were qualified using the pool. Enrollees of Company 1491 were noted for their energy and spirit.

Company 1446, Camp F-3, Alexandria—One of 10 Louisiana companies to be conditioned at Fort Benning, GA, Company 1446 was organized June 21, 1933. It was assigned a site at Castor Plunge, about 14 miles southwest of Alexandria, LA. Castor Plunge was noted for its spring-fed swimming pool that was a local attraction. It was a National forest camp, and its work assignment related to reforestation and protection from wildfires. CCC crews in Camp F-3 had the distinction of

never having to live in tents. Barracks and wooden huts that held about six enrollees were used for housing until additional barracks were constructed.

Fire preventative efforts were high on the list of assignments for the men of Company 1446. In 1937, Company 1446 set up 156 miles of fire breaks, built 24 miles of high-service and 35 miles of low-service roads, erected two 100-foot steel fire towers, and installed 48 miles of telephone lines that connected these facilities. To facilitate reforestation efforts, CCC crews built 70 miles of fences that surrounded 22,900 acres. By 1937, the CCC crews had planted over 17,000 acres with pine seedlings amounting to over 15 million seedlings within these planting areas.

Another major project was development of the Valentine Lake Recreational Area, a 65-acre lake formed by the 500-foot dam the Camp F-3 CCC crews built. The Camp F-3 CCC workers also built 75 picnic tables, 35 fire places, 2 boat docks, 2 rafts, a registration booth, a bath house, and an athletic field for the recreational area (U.S. Army

Building the dam for the Valentine Lake Recreational Area near Gardner was a major accomplishment.

1937). The development of the Valentine Lake area was a significant accomplishment and a lasting contribution to the residents of central Louisiana, including families who visit the lake for swimming, canoeing, and fishing.

Company 1446 CCC workers took advantage of a multitude of educational opportunities, including courses in elementary school-level subjects through the third grade as well as in more advanced subjects, such as citizenship, etiquette, journalism, typing, safety, first aid, lifesaving, baking and cooking, auto mechanics, woodworking, carpentry, painting, photography, forestry, and vocational subjects related to the work project.

Facilities at Camp F-3 were good, with a mess hall and kitchen that provided and served good food. Meals at holidays such as Thanksgiving were special, and local community leaders were invited to participate. The CCC camps trained cooks and bakers, as well as stewards who served meals.

The CCC workers were responsible for keeping their uniforms clean and weekends were often a time for washing their clothes. In an oral history captured by Anna

Burns (2000a), a CCC worker named Otis Miller describes how he washed clothes for others on weekends for 25 cents:

I got a sideline and it was washing. I'd go down to the creek right behind the camp where the same water that goes through the Castor Plunge creek, and I'd get soap and washing powder out of the kitchen, and take it to the creek. I had some 55-gallon drums I'd cut down and that was my wash pots. I'd build a fire under that.

I didn't even have a rub-board. They had some old stiff brushes, but I didn't even use that. I got me a big old heavy board, and laid it on two logs, and I'd pound those clothes with a limb, and stir them and wash them and boil that water. I didn't just let it get hot; I'd boil that water. After they got clean, of course, the dirt and sweat was all you wanted out of them anyway. The blue came out whether you wanted it to or not. They call them blue jeans today.

Camp F-3 published a newspaper called *The Camp Packard Leader*, and some Company 1446 CCC workers participated in glee club singing and a string band organized by the company commander's wife. These musical groups broadcast each Saturday over radio station KALB in Alexandria, LA.

Thanksgiving Dinner 1934

Camp Packard Company, 1446-F3
Alexandria, La.

Menus for Thanksgiving meals at Civilian Conservation Corps camps indicate that a special effort went into making these memorable.

A close bond developed between many of the military officers, user agency foremen, and the CCC workers. Joseph M. Berry, a worker assigned to Camp Packard in 1937, worked in the camp as a truck driver for several months and, then, while still assigned to Company 1446, was moved to Camp Beauregard and became the driver for Major N.B. Bush, the District E Executive Officer. Bush had a great deal of confidence in Berry, and at the end of Berry's enrollment in 1939, Bush presented him with a wrist watch. This act made a tremendous impression on Berry, and he recalled this act fondly almost 60 years later (Burns 1998).

Upon the closure of Camp F-3 in October 1938, Company 1446 was transferred to Hackberry to establish Camp BF-1.

Companies 276 and 5405, Camp F-4, Leesville—

Company 276, composed of enrollees from New York and New Jersey, was established in the fall of 1933 about 15 miles southeast of Leesville and named Camp Vernon. CCC crews from Companies 276 constructed roads, firebreaks, and bridges, and planted trees. When the enrollment of most of the men of Company 276 ended in early 1935, Company 5405 was established to replace it. Organized in Rome, GA, on August 7, 1935, Company 5405 consisted of 200 CCC workers who traveled to Leesville to reestablish Camp Vernon. The Georgia crews fit into the camp life well and were soon accepted by the residents of Leesville and DeRidder. Over time, most of the Georgia contingent left to return home, find employment, or get married, and local enrollees filled the ranks of the company.

The work assignment for Company 5405 was forestry, primarily fire prevention and suppression as well as tree planting. Most of the local CCC workers had a keen personal interest in the forestry work, because, as one worker stated, "We live near here, and for miles around here the land is barren as a result of the ruthless cutting of pine trees. Someday the work we are doing here is going to pay us far greater dividends than the pay we now get" (U.S. Army 1939).

CCC crews from Company 5405 planted more than 24 million pine seedlings in an area of about 20,000 acres, while keeping watch over an area of about 108,000 acres.

BELOW: Civilian Conservation Corps workers plant pine seedlings in the barren landscape typical of southwest Louisiana in the 1930s. RIGHT: Many miles of fencing were built by Civilian Conservation Corps workers in forestry camps to protect newly planted seedlings.

The crews built 65 miles of pasture fencing, 40 miles of hard surface roads, and 150 miles of travelable firebreaks.

In an addition to the regular work assignments, a side, or spike, camp was located 17 miles from the main site near Camp Claiborne. Side camps were authorized to work on projects distant from the main camp that could be handled by a cadre of about 25 enrollees. Typically, crews of side camps operated out of tents with supervision from the user agency. The mission of the side camp from Camp Vernon is not well understood, but it seems related to animal husbandry. CCC workers in the Camp Vernon side camp oversaw the raising of 117 chickens. Three side camp workers studied swine husbandry and managed a swine herd of 12 pigs, and several workers tended the camp's garden (U.S. Army 1939).

To increase the effectiveness of the work assigned, each worker received 2 weeks of instruction in the "why and wherefore" of the project by the Project Superintendent A.S. Warner and members of the Forest Service.

Most Camp Vernon buildings were replaced in the fall of 1938 with a new generation of prefabricated facilities, including a recreation hall and a dispensary that were described as the best of their kind in the district.

All of the workers engaged in educational activities, with popular classes in first aid, typing, agriculture, leadership training, and auto mechanics. Several workers took college-level classes in subjects such as English and trigonometry. John Hunter, educational advisor for the camp in 1939, was uncertain of the camp's achievement

in education when he left the CCC, but later realized that the camp had accomplished much more than he at first had thought. Teaching men how to read and write and upgrading the level of education of all workers were important accomplishments, Hunter saw, and he praised the leadership and instruction given to the enrollees by the military and forestry employees at Camp Vernon (Humphreys 1964a).

The Leesville camp had a keen intramural athletic competition between barracks. It also boasted a five-man swing band that broadcast its music throughout the camp nightly, a stunt night, and a safety suggestion box that received frequent use (U.S. Army 1939).

Companies 255 and 5406, Camp F-5, Dry Prong— Camp F-5, established in the fall of 1933 by Company 255, was made up of enrollees from New York and New Jersey. The workers developed the camp 6 miles north of Dry Prong and began the forestry related activities of planting seedlings, building roads and bridges, installing telephone line, and joined with workers from Camp F-1 on construction of the Stuart Nursery lake dam.

Camp F-5 was rather isolated and entertainment was mostly self-generated. At Christmas time, however, Mary Leeper of Alexandria unofficially joined the company as an entertainer, leading each Monday evening, through her spirited playing on the piano, a contingent of CCC workers who sang and played their instruments. From time to time, she invited blues singers, banjo players, readers, dancers, and other entertainers to camp. From her efforts emerged the camp song "Hail, Hail to Dry Prong,"

TOP: *Camp F-5 was built a few miles north of Dry Prong by enrollees from New York and New Jersey. These Civilian Conservation Corps workers were transferred to California in 1935 and then men from Louisiana were assigned to the camp.* BOTTOM: *Road and partially completed bridge constructed over Iatt Creek by Camp 5406 enrollees.*

composed by Al Lewis, a former company baker. The song was sung lustily on any and all occasions (U.S. Army 1934).

Company 5406, organized in August 1935, replaced Company 255, which was transferred to California. The inception of Company 5406, made up of enrollees from Georgia, Florida, and Louisiana, coincided with significant improvements to life on the camp, including food served on tables in the mess hall, a recreation room, and expansion of the first-aid room into an infirmary. Camp F-5 was closed sometime during 1936; it does not appear in the 1937 annual report.

Company 5407, Camp F-6, Winnfield—Camp F-6 was built in late 1934 by Company 277 a mile north of Calvin, LA. Company 277 was transferred to Salinas, CA, in 1935, and Company 5407 was organized in August 1935 with 200 enrollees from Georgia. The military staff of Company 5407 made improvement of camp facilities a priority: problems with the campsite's storm water drainage were addressed, the kitchen was updated, and a barber shop was built.

Under an extensive athletic program, Company 5407 boasted a crackerjack cadre of basketball players, boxers, and baseball players. In the fall of 1937, Company 5407

The Gum Springs swimming area was a very popular addition to the Winnfield area.

won several championships in independent tournaments. One worker attended college on a scholarship based on his basketball prowess, and another worker, while attending Calvin High School, made the all-State basketball team and then obtained a college scholarship when the high school won the Class B State championship (U.S. Army 1939).

But whether they were involved in sports or not, almost all of the Company 5407 CCC workers were involved in the Camp F-6 educational program, with several attending high school and two on leave from the CCC to attend college. An unusual aspect of the educational program of Company 5407 was a class on bee culture. Camp F-6 had four bee hives, and many of the camp's CCC workers became involved in collecting more hives.

Project work assigned to the CCC workers of Camp F-6 included building forest roads, fencing of plantations, ridding the area of hogs, fighting fire, preparing fire presuppression, building telephone lines, and planting pine seedlings. To make the project work more effective, a side, or spike, camp was established under the supervision of Sam Whitener, a foreman who oversaw the work of 37 workers on additional projects miles away from the main camp.

In addition to the usual forestry projects, CCC workers from Company 5407 worked on a number of projects for the local area, including development of a recreational park near the Gum Springs fire tower on the Natchitoches-Winnfield highway. CCC workers from Company 5407 built the park's parking area, picnic tables and benches, barbecue pits, playground, and swimming area.

Company 4406, Camp F-7, Chestnut—Company 4406, organized in June 1935, was situated on a hill about 3 miles east of Chestnut (today Chestnut is a small unorganized community south of Saline) with enrollees who came primarily from northern Louisiana. Through a concerted effort on part of both the military officers and user agency employees, the CCC workers made Camp F-7 one of the most outstanding camps of the district.

Under management of the using service (the Forest Service), CCC crews from Company 4406 improved the area's roads, installed telephone lines, upgraded recreational facilities along Saline Bayou, worked on protecting forest land, and offered instruction to local citizens on fire protection.

Under the educational program started in November 1935 by J.H. Alexander, the Camp F-7 educational advisor, the men of Company 4406 could learn about everything from the typical elementary and high school curriculum of the time to more advanced undertakings, including vocational training, drama, music, and personal development.

Camp F-7 presumably closed in 1936, based on the absence of records of the camp in the army's 1937 annual report.

Company 1477, Camp F-8, Pollock—Company 1477 was organized at Fort Barrancas, FL, on April 28, 1933, and established Camp F-2 12 miles south of Provencal. After about 2 years of work in road building and forest maintenance, the company was reassigned, and on June 4, 1935, Company 1477 moved to a site near Pollock, about

TOP LEFT: *One of several fire lookout towers constructed by Company 5407.* TOP RIGHT: *Recreational facilities were developed along Saline Bayou.* BOTTOM: *Civilian Conservation Corps truck equipped with firefighting equipment was one maintained by the camp. Note the Civilian Conservation Corps plate on the bed that reads, "This driver is requested to drive carefully."*

half a mile from the Stuart Nursery—one of the largest pine nurseries in the United States. Company 1477, named Camp Taylor after U.S. President Zachary Taylor, provided the manpower to maintain and operate the nursery as well as carry out other assignments as needed. Camp F-8, on 20 acres of rolling hills, featured a nicely landscaped site where buildings were well spaced. The site, its facilities, and leadership of the military officers and user agency foremen made the enrollees willing workers with a high level of esprit de corps.

The CCC workers of Company 1477 were the caretakers of 25 million seedlings yearly. They also handled all the motor repair work for the trucks, ambulances, and passenger vehicles in District E, and they hosted the District E Cooking School—all work that gave Company 1477 special distinction in the annals of CCC work.

The nursery work in itself was monumental. The CCC workers of Company 1477 received practical training in the gathering of pine cones, processing cones and

TOP: Civilian Conservation Corps crews weed beds of loblolly pine seedlings at Stuart Nursery. This was a time-consuming task, but only one of many activities needed to produce 25 million southern pine seedlings each year. BOTTOM LEFT: The Southern Forest Experiment Station office and laboratory at Stuart Nursery. BOTTOM RIGHT: The visitor center for the Big Creek Recreation Camp that was developed by Company 1477.

seeds with techniques to maintain a high level of seed viability, seeding technology, seedling culture, and lifting and storing seedlings were provided to the enrollees. In addition to the supervision of the nursery manager, A.D. Reed, the Southern Forest Experiment Station maintained a staff of nursery scientists, led by M.A. Huberman. This research did much to optimize seedling production. Company 1477 CCC crews had the opportunity to interact and work with the nursery scientists.

Planting of seedlings was a major assignment for the CCC workers on all Forest Service camps. Most of the Forest Service land acquired for the Kisatchie National Forest had been clearcut by previous owners, so reforestation was a significant responsibility. Southern Forest Experiment Station scientists at the nursery on Camp F-8 directed the planting of nearly 750,000 seedlings in research studies on the Palustris Experimental Forest, which had been created on the Evangeline Ranger District. CCC workers from Company 1477 played a role not only in growing and planting trees but also in the development of the nursery technology used across the South in reforestation

efforts. This information is documented in P.C. Wakeley's "Planting the Southern Pines," a book which also provided the framework for post-World War II nursery operations (Wakeley 1954).

Along with their nursery responsibilities, the CCC workers of Company 1477 carried out the routine forestry program of fire prevention, firefighting, and building and maintaining roads, and the workers led the development of a wildlife preserve, which required the use of a side camp on U.S. Highway 167 near Dry Prong (U.S. Army 1939).

Local skilled auto mechanics managed the Central Motor Repair Shop at Camp F-8, with a group of 36 CCC workers cross-trained from preliminary duties of truck washing and greasing to maintaining intricate engine adjustments. Many of these workers later secured excellent jobs in automobile repair after leaving the CCC.

One of the community projects the CCC crews from Camp F-8 undertook was to develop a recreation center at Big Creek Camp, complete with 20 barbecue pits, picnic tables, and swimming and fishing improvements. In addition, an amphitheater seating 2,000 was constructed by the CCC crews where movies were shown weekly. This made the camp an integral part of the community.

Camp F-8 CCC workers studied under the tutelage of Hubert H. Beal, camp educational advisor, in a well-lit education building that housed 3,000 books and featured linoleum flooring and modern, comfortable chairs.

The District Cooking School at Camp F-8 trained incoming officers, cooks, and mess stewards from other camps on how to cut meat, cook, and bake as well as on the sanitation, menu preparation, and record keeping required in the operation of an army mess.

Camp F-8 was an important camp in District E and well deserved the awards and accolades that it received.

P—Private Land, Division of Forestry, Louisiana Department of Conservation

On April 6, 1933, State Forester V.H. Sonderegger represented Louisiana at a meeting in Washington, DC, to discuss allocation of CCC companies to Louisiana. He received an assignment of 23 camps for establishment on State and private forest land in the State. In addition to the CCC enrollees, 300 men 25 years of age or older who had experience in woods work were authorized. These local experienced men (LEMs) were to be recruited as foremen of CCC camp crews.

In addition to the 23 camps already in place across Louisiana, four more camps were established in the State through temporary transfers from western States, where extreme winter weather had made work and living conditions difficult. Sixteen of the camps were assigned to forestry; 14 of these were located on private land. Two other camps were located on State owned or controlled lands—the State Forest at Woodworth and Allen Northwest Game Refuge near Winnfield, although no camp was developed for the game refuge.

On the 14 camps on private land in Louisiana, work consisted entirely of forest fire protection, construction of roads and fire breaks through the forest, fire hazard reduction, telephone line construction, and erection of fire lookout towers. In accordance with Forest Service instructions, the CCC could work only on private lands that participated in the Clarke-McNary program, under which landowners contributed two cents per acre annually to the Division of Forestry for fire protection (Sonderegger 1934). Planting of trees was not a part of the Clarke-McNary program.

The CCC completed a tremendous amount of forestry-related work under the sponsorship of the Division of

Forestry. State Forester Sonderegger reported that the work program of the CCC included constructing aids for firefighting, construction of administration buildings, nursery and reforestation work, and actual firefighting. Under the category of controlling wildfires, Louisiana's CCC crews built 31 fire towers, 10 tower residences, 2,998 bridges, 2,142 miles of telephone lines, 63 cattle guards, and 3,070 miles of truck trails (Burns 1968).

State Forester V.H. Sonderegger had responsibility for forestry camps on private lands.

About 20 camps were established under the supervision of the Division of Forestry. Many of these were closed within 2 years after completing their assigned tasks. Sufficient information is not available to provide a history of each camp, but the following sections offer a description of State forestry camp programs and their missions and accomplishments.

In additional to the forestry camps discussed here, the Division of Forestry, Department of Conservation, established camps in Montgomery, Springville, Danville, Sikes, Ansley, Marion, Greensburg, Elizabeth, Chatham, Winnfield, Grangeville, and Robeline.

Company 1493, Camp P-51, Bogalusa—Among the first CCC camps established on private forest lands was Camp P-51 near Bogalusa on a tract of land owned by the Great Southern Lumber Company. On May 23, 1933, Company 1493 came into being with the induction of 187 CCC enrollees. Other enrollees were added to bring the company to full strength at 200 workers. The camp was named Camp Maestri in honor of Robert S. Maestri, head of the Louisiana Department of Conservation.

When the enrollees, under the command of Capt. W.A. Mett, Jr., arrived by train, officials of Great Southern Lumber Company and local citizens were on hand to welcome and help the group. In a few hours, 30 tents were raised and other work was under way to make the camp livable. Dedication of the camp was held in October with ceremony participants including local civic organizations, along with many regional, State, and local officials. The camp site was moved in January 1935 to 9 miles northeast of Bogalusa.

Typical of the work on many of the forestry camps sponsored by the Division of Forestry, the mission, activities, and accomplishments of the CCC crews of Camp

LEFT: *Fighting fire by hand, and with few tools, was common early in the program, but techniques improved with time.*
RIGHT: *Constructing and manning fire lookout towers did much to reduce losses from fire and improve forest management.*
BOTTOM: *Construction of roads such as this one did much to improve access for fire protection activities.*

P-51 were focused on bringing knowledge of forestry and conservation to the Louisiana. Fire protection was the work assigned to the camp, and, with an ever increasing distance from the camp, the CCC workers undertook the work of building firebreaks, lanes, truck roads and trails, telephone lines, observation towers, and other protective measures.

The School of Forestry at Louisiana State University (LSU) owned and operated its school forest near Camp P-51. Professors and students from the LSU School Forest provided CCC workers with instruction on practical and modern methods of forest management.

Wildfires and their devastating effects became firmly fixed in the minds of the CCC workers assigned to Camp

P-51, when, on Easter Sunday of 1934, fires spread across 1,200 acres of forest near the camp. Through improved methods of fire detection and thanks to the experience of the CCC workers in applying the new methods, the CCC crews greatly reduced the number of acres that otherwise might have gone up in flame. Reductions in fire losses resulted from a Camp Efficiency Program that awarded inducements and privileges to camp crews with the quickest average fire response times. Among those who were appreciative of Camp P-51's heightened level of fire protection were the owners and managers of the Great Southern Lumber Company, who documented their appreciation in letters of commendation for the work of the CCC firefighters (U.S. Army 1937).

Company 2428, Camp P-52, Slidell—Camp Sonderegger, officially known as Camp P-52, was established by an advance group of veterans in July 1933. Just on the outskirts of Slidell, Camp P-52 was nestled in a beautiful pine grove not far from Lake Pontchartrain. One of the oldest and finest camps in the district, Camp Sonderegger was developed by experienced craftsmen of various skills, including expert draftsmen, architects, engineers, carpenters, brick and stone masons, and others of the buildings trades.

Among the 200 men who made up the roster of Company 2428 were many whose homes were nearby. Nearly half of the company's workers lived in New Orleans and could look forward to frequent visits to their families.

Over a 4-year period, Camp P-52 CCC workers built about 120 miles of truck trails, installed 175 miles of telephone lines, constructed 1,200 miles of fire lanes and breaks, and erected 4 lookout towers. As a result, fires could be spotted from towers and reported by telephone with exact location identified on a map, and within 5 minutes, a fire fighting team could be on the way—giving the area a capability that significantly reduced its risk of timber losses from wildfire.

In July 1934, a side camp was established at the site of an old logging camp near Tailsheek, about 25 miles north of Slidell. The side camp expanded to include a group of small barracks, a recreation hall, an office building, a first-aid building, and officers' quarters. The site was dominated by a fire tower from which a constant lookout was maintained. The size of the side camp increased to 75 enrollees (U.S. Army 1937).

The educational program at Company 2428 was devoted to practical training that included boat building, furniture repair, camp development, and various skill sets used in operating camp equipment and managing camp facilities. The educational program also included a library service in an arrangement with the Louisiana Library Commission and the New Orleans public library.

Among pleasant memories noted by the CCC workers of Camp P-52 were dances, indoor games, contributions from Red Cross and Disabled Veterans organizations, band concerts, and holiday dinners.

Company 1495, Camp P-66, Jena/Olla—On May 3, 1933, 53 men were selected for the startup of a new company. They received their conditioning training at Camp Beauregard, where they remained until June 28. Under the leadership of Capt. S.A. Hall, the CCC enrollees assisted the army with the processing 1,600 CCC recruits. In mid-June, a cadre of 89 men was assigned to the company. Later in June, another 17 men from Fort Barrancas joined the group. These 17 enrollees were originally from New Orleans, and most were prize fighters, which helped later in athletic competitions.

On June 28, Company 1495 was transported to the camp site known as Nickels Springs, about 14 miles north of Jena. The site was a small ridge of land near the spring, which became the water supply for the camp. Camp P-66 was dubbed Camp Swan after E.L Swan, president of the Southern Kraft Paper Company, in Bastrop, LA, who managed the lands where the camp's CCC crews carried out their forestry responsibilities.

By July, Camp Swan had its own column in the local newspaper *Jena Times*. The column, titled "Tom Cat's Column…Interesting bits of news and nonsense from CCC Camp #1495," included announcements of upcoming dances, such as one that was held in Jena with the Dixie Music Makers, an African-American jazz band (Willis 2001).

Beginning in August 1933, the CCC crews of Company 1495 began work in road construction, and, over the next 2 years, built about 250 bridges, 375 culverts, 106 miles of telephone lines, and 240 miles of truck trails. They also contributed about 7,000 workdays of forest firefighting.

One of the most outstanding accomplishments in the history of Camp Swan was the part that CCC workers played in the 1937 Flood Relief work in the Black River area. Records indicate that the CCC workers from Camp Swan helped transport 1,215 families and their household goods, 19,794 farm animals, 250 loads of water (for refugees), and 158 truckloads of feed stuff. Not one personal injury occurred among the refugees while being transported in CCC trucks. The camp's CCC workers put 2,629 workdays into this effort. Capt. E.C. Fleming, Camp Commanding Officer, and Robert W. Human, Project Superintendent, were in charge of CCC involvement in the flood relief work (U.S. Army 1937).

Camp Swan's educational program included courses in public speaking, etiquette, typing, first aid, woodworking, radio, and elementary classes. The camp also held cooking classes with participation from seven other CCC camps.

Company 1492, Camp P-58, Olla/Urania—Company 1492 was organized at Camp Beauregard on May 18, 1933, and moved to the site outside Olla and near Urania in June. Named in honor of Henry E. Hardtner, of the Urania Lumber Company, the camp was soon recognized as the best in District E. Hardtner, who had done much to promote the practice of forestry in the South, was well recognized as a leader in forest industry. In a speech at the dedication of the camp on September 14, 1933, Hardtner voiced approval of the southern pine industry for President Roosevelt's reforestation program, praising the work of the young men of the CCC:

Civilian Conservation Corps workers on horseback herding cattle to high ground as result of the 1937 flood. (Photograph from State Library of Louisiana archives).

What means this army of some 300,000 of our best young men in the U.S. Conservation Camps...? This army of young men will receive $5,000,000 or more for their services, and they are earning every cent paid them. As a relief measure alone, as some term it, over 2,000,000 people are directly benefited, for these boys send home to their families the greater part of their wages... Their association and work in the forests for six months or more give them an intimate knowledge of forestry—they are taught in a practical way the problems of forestry... So in short space of a year our population of 120,000,000 people are educated to forestry and become forest-minded. Such an accomplishment at so slight a cost is almost miraculous and only a Roosevelt, endowed with wisdom by Almighty God, could have been brave enough and strong enough to undertake such an herculean task (Humphreys 1964b).

Hardtner's speech, giving support to the CCC and its forestry program, was well received in Washington, DC. The Southern Pine Association requested several thousand copies of the speech, and CCC leaders directed that the speech be read to the assembled companies in all CCC camps and that copies would be placed in all CCC camp libraries.

Camp P-58 was responsible for some 300,000 acres of forest land, of which about 220,000 acres were under management of the Clarke-McNary Program and thus eligible for CCC involvement. The largest landowner of this area was the Urania Lumber Company, and about 100 experimental plots of the Southern Forest Experiment Station and Yale University also were close to the Camp P-58 campsite. Camp P-58 CCC workers built 400 miles of truck trails, installed 150 miles of telephone lines, and constructed some 1,200 bridges and culverts. All these efforts were an important part of reducing wildfire losses.

Camp P-58's educational advisor developed a well-rounded educational program the workers, many of whom had not completed elementary school. The program grew to 15 different subjects and an enrollment of 45 workers who learned to read and write. Camp P-58 educational facilities included a large building that housed an auditorium, modern library, classrooms, drawing room, and advisor's office.

The camp was of great benefit to the men of Company 1492 as well as to the families and parents of the men, and certainly, too, the community gained much from the work accomplished by Company 1492's CCC workers.

L—Levee Roads, Louisiana State Board of Engineers

Closely related to the CCC program's drainage projects and to the Soil Conservation Service's watershed projects were the large flood control projects undertaken by the U.S.

Henry Hardtner, a strong advocate of forestry.

29

Army Corps of Engineers. Under the 1933 Unemployment Relief Act, the president of the United States could extend CCC services to "such works as necessary in the public interest to control floods." Under this provision, Harry Jacobs, State Engineer for the Louisiana Board of Engineers, applied to Robert Fechner, Director of the CCC, for approval of CCC work on projects to construct 600 to 700 miles of dirt roads "parallel with and contiguous to existing levee lines" along the Mississippi River and its tributaries in Louisiana (Humphreys 1964a). Most of this work necessarily had to be accomplished by hand labor.

Many of roads and highways ran a distance of 5 to 10 miles from levee lines. During floods, many of the breaks in levees resulted from an inability to promptly reach threatened areas with adequate material and labor. The State Board of Engineers was confident that an adequate system of secondary roads would reduce the cost of levee maintenance and supervision and at the same time would increase the protection of life and property (Humphreys 1964a).

CCC crews from four camps were given work on the levee projects. The projects were assigned to the Department of Conservation and then reassigned to the State Board of Engineers. In addition to the usual group of supervisory men assigned to the CCC camps, the engineers placed a group of their own men familiar with road construction in the camps. The payroll and supporting equipment for these extra men was furnished by the CCC program. These levee camps were the only ones in the national CCC program. The camps were located where the State Board of Engineers considered the need for building roads adjacent to levees the most urgent (Humphreys 1964a).

Company 1480, Camp L-64, Sherburne—CCC workers from Camp Sherburne, on the east bank of the Atchafalaya River, were given the task of completing 24.7 miles of road along the levee along with the requisite fence relocation and drainage work. The CCC crew was made up of 204 African-American workers and the typical assignment of military leadership. The development and work of Camp Sherburne can best be described by one of the CCC workers, Archie Long (U.S. Army 1934):

We arrived in camp about 4:00 o'clock on the hot afternoon of June 29, 1933. It was a disgusting scene, the site picked by Lt. Burnham. A spot located near the village of Sherburne, on the banks of the Atchafalaya River, three miles from a railroad station.

The dream of every one (except the officers who knew better) was a well-constructed camp, cold showers, supper on arrival, etc. But to our utmost disappointment, we saw a deserted dairy barn, tall grass, snakes, mosquitoes, pole cats, and no water for drinking, much less showers.

Most of us from New Orleans thought of turning around and going back home. We were not accustomed to this camp life, and felt it was fit for country folks only.

Hard work and good food developed strong bodies.

Under the strenuous supervision of the officers, enlisted men and the older boys with leadership, we got busy clearing off space to sleep, pitched tents and hauled water from the village to get supper cooked. A snake killed, a pole cat chased, the discovering of a wasp nest and such things created big excitement among us city boys, which helped us to forget about going home.

Darkness came along before we were issued a mosquito bar. Each man had to build his own mosquito bar rack by the light of a candle, with only a couple of hammers to be used by the whole company. All that night practical jokers were at their old tricks. At a wee hour in the morning cries came from a group of boys that a bear was in camp. One boy swore that he actually saw a bear, and hit him on the back with a stick. This brought the officers to our aid with guns, but no bear was to be found. I still say that the bear in camp that night was the big furry hound that's been hanging around camp since that day. But you can be sure that every tent side was tied down close to the ground from that moment to sunrise.

Sunrise and everyone was up bright and early. After breakfast, a lecture from our C.O. gave us new hope.

The next few days were spent clearing off more space, lining up tents, and leveling the camp ground. At first the job was hard, harder than most of us had ever done. But as the days went by, the work and well-balanced food strengthened and prepared us for the next job outlined by higher authorities. This job is 23 miles of levee road to be built with wheelbarrows and shovels. Seven miles of this road has been built.

The old dairy barn has been cleaned out, and we are now using it along with two new barracks for sleeping quarters. A main mess hall for enrollees has been built, a log cabin for the C.O., and officers' mess, camp headquarters, foresters' headquarters, officers' sleeping quarters, and forester sleeping quarters.

The President states our time is about up now, and every period new members are coming in, replacing old members with prospects of getting a job.

Our greatest regret will be leaving our C.O., Lt. S.A. Martin, who along with Lt. G.J. Loupret, our former C.O., we owe the camp's great success. It was a camp with a clean record from start to finish. Now we are leaving the dream of everyone, a well-constructed camp, which consists of comfortable sleeping quarters, hot or cold showers, light plant, a wonderful bunch of officers, and an unbeaten baseball team.... How I shall hate to leave.

After Company 1480 completed its work of building 24.7 miles of roads with fence relocation and drainage improvements in December 1934, the company moved to the Louisiana town of New Roads to build more levee roads.

Company 1480, Camp L-72, New Roads—In October 1934, anticipating a move to Camp L-72 near New Roads, Company 1480 took on a cadre of men from Sherburne to develop camp facilities in the New Roads area. In December, the entire company moved to the new site, where the company's assignment was to construct 6.9 miles of highway along levees around Bayou Sara Point and Point Menior.

An aggressive educational program for the CCC workers of Camp L-72 offered classes in elementary education and high school subjects, and included private and group tutoring.

The camp distinguished itself by well-kept grounds and a cooperative attitude among all the CCC workers, the military cadre, and the professional staffs. The work of this camp was completed in the fall of 1936.

Company 1481, Camp L-61, Krotz Springs— Company 1481, established in June 1933 at Fort Barrancas, FL, consisted of 206 African-American enrollees who set up camp at Krotz Springs on June 29, 1933, along the Atchafalaya River. So mosquito infested and swampy was

Levee road construction work was difficult. Enrollees worked under harsh conditions and built without use of earth-moving equipment.

the site that after a few weeks camp leaders deemed it necessary to move Camp L-61 to another site one-half mile west of Krotz Springs.

As the task of finishing the development of the camp progressed, Camp L-61 CCC workers began their road construction work on the 21.8 mile Melville-Krotz Springs levee road, where they went on to move 136,444 cubic yards of earth and establish ditches and culverts. The commanding officer, Capt. Frank A. Hemphill, was an avid sports enthusiast who gave full support to the camp's diversified educational activities and sports programs. This boosted morale among Camp L-61 workers, who worked so quickly on building the Atchafalaya River levee roads that their work was completed in the spring of 1935.

Company 1481, Camp L-73, Marksville—On completion of the Melville-Krotz Springs levee road by Camp L-61, Company 1481 was transferred to a site near the village of Moncla, about 6 miles north of Marksville where Camp L-61 was established in May 1935.

After Camp L-61, CCC workers completed 6.2 miles of highway construction on the south bank of the Red River from Echo to Moncla, and from Barbin's Landing to Lake Long, the camp closed in February 1936.

Company 1488, Camp L-56, LaPlace—Company 1488 started up on June 3, 1933, when the first detachment of enrollees arrived at Fort Barrancas, FL. After a few days, the company obtained full strength of 200 enrollees and was placed under the command of Capt. J.C. Horan from Mississippi State College.

CCC worker Louis "Pee Wee" Ellis wrote the following description of the company's experience in developing and working at L-56 near LaPlace (U.S. Army 1934):

TOP: *Work crew of Civilian Conservation Corps enrollees taking a break from road construction for a photo. (Photo: National Archives).* LEFT: *Civilian Conservation Corps camp barracks typical of the wooden structures that replaced the temporary tent housing in most all camps.*

After conditioning was completed and all equipment was drawn, the company entrained at Pensacola for "Bonnett Carre Spillway," somewhere in Louisiana. Where? None of us were able to find out until a fellow enrollee was located who lived in the vicinity of the said spillway. The information received from him only heightened our anxiety as to the kind of place we were to inhabit.

Lt. D.J. MacCalman, U.S. Navy, had preceded the company to LaPlace to arrange for a camp site and make other arrangements that were necessary before the arrival of the company. We landed in the back yard of a lumber company and proceeded to eat our dinner. Next came the hike to our future home. Not so encouraging at the first sight, but after all the tents had been pitched and some brush hooks had been at work, we could all see the foresight which our "advance guard" had shown.

After a couple of months of hectic work and many mistakes, camp life finally lost its novelty and settled down to the grind of everyday existence. Tanned bodies became the mark of distinction among the men. Wheelbarrows and shovels became more fitted to our hands and were not looked upon with great disfavor by the most of us. Those who did not belong were weeded out and given free transportation.

Dances, basketball, baseball, tennis, football, and other forms of amusement were provided and the camp began to be more like home. Upon the detachment of Capt. Horan, Lt. MacCalman took command and has done everything possible, with the assistance of Lt. L.E. Davis and Mr. J.W. Openwayer, superintendent, to make this camp one of the best in the district.

With the arrival of new men every few months and discharge of many of our friends to take jobs on the *outside, the company does not have the same appearance that was noticeable in the first days of its existence. The original members can usually be picked by their bearing and by their actions, both social and workaday.*

As our camp has a feature that none of the other camps in this district, and probably any other can boast, a description seems to be in order. After leaving LaPlace by the way of the old Jefferson Davis Highway for New Orleans, the levee is crossed about a half mile from LaPlace. Upon crossing the levee a most surprising scene meets the eye. Situated on the batture is Camp L-56 overlooking the ole Mississippi River. With beautiful lawns and buildings painted green, our camp makes an appearance that is hard to beat. Of course, the Mississippi makes a good swimming hole.

The work of Camp L-56 consisted of constructing roads that would feature a 24-foot crown, built slightly above the seep line, along the levees on both sides of the Bonnett Carre Spillway. The use of ballast gravel from an abandoned railroad embankment on the spillway permitted surfacing of most the road with no additional cost. Camp L-56 CCC workers, using wheelbarrows and shovels, built 13.6 miles of roads, 50 percent of which was graveled. Camp L-56 closed February 10, 1936.

Company 1487, Camp L-70, St. Joseph—The
camp near St. Joseph, in Tensas Parish, was organized in July 1933. The assignment for Camp L-70 was to construct 15.6 miles of road that would feature a 24-foot crown and the requisite culverts and drainage ditches, a job that entailed handling 104,441 cubic yards of soil and relocating and rebuilding many miles of farm fencing.

Enrollee Willard Y. Cuney provided the following description of camp establishment (U.S. Army 1934):

Under the command of Capt. D.W. South, Jr., Camp L-70 was started on the twenty-seventh day of May 1933, 5 miles from the little town of St. Joseph. It was made up of boys from the following places: New Orleans, Lafayette, Shreveport, and local boys.

We arrived in the night of the twenty-sixth of May, hungry and tired. We were given a small box containing an apple and a few sandwiches. This was only a bite for us hungry boys who had been used to a square meal. A passenger coach was what we had to sleep in that night, what little sleep we got.

After about three days the camp was in good enough condition so that work of building a road along the levee was begun. Now this is the time that quite a few fellows went "over the hill" because sleeping in cramped quarters, have to eat in the open, sleeping with mosquitoes swarming around, combined with the road work, the boys thought that they could make it better elsewhere, so about 40 went "over the hill."

In the months of September and August, the camp had to be moved to the shore of Lake Bruen about a mile farther

Civilian Conservation Corps men working with hand tools to construct many miles of roads along levees in Louisiana.

FAR LEFT: A portion of Company 1487 at L-70, St. Joseph, LA, commanded by U.S. Navy Lt. George Walker.
LEFT: Camp sports activities provided an excellent opportunity for men from rural areas to develop social skills.
BELOW: The company's baseball and other sports teams were named after the camp's site location at Lake Bruen in Louisiana.

from the old camp. This new camp site was all grown up in weeds and bushes and had to be cleared up before trying to start building. This was accomplished within a few days and everything was all set for building the mess hall, this was constructed first.

This was about the time that Capt. Smith was relieved by Lt. George Walker, U.S. Navy, who took command. Lt. Walker took charge of everything and work was begun on the barracks.

It was the latter part of October that the camp was completed. Recreation hall, mess hall, five barracks, plus the officers' quarters completed the camp.

On December 5, 1933, about 30 new enrollees came in from Baton Rouge and Lake Arthur. After this, sports and schooling was started on a small scale. Baseball and boxing teams were organized.

Mr. Tinnin of the Panama Canal Zone arrived in camp to take the duties of educational advisor on the first of May. He re-organized the night classes, promoted different kinds of educational activities that proved valuable to the men in camp. He has organized a dramatic club that is gaining popularity rapidly in this section of the country.

Much to our sorrow, we are losing our commanding officer, Lt. George Walker. He is being relieved by Capt. Stearn, who has had command of a camp in North Carolina. We feel that he will make a good commanding officer and we wish Lt. Walker the best of luck in later life.

So, let me conclude by saying that the men in Company 1487, St. Joseph, LA, sincerely believe that we have one of the best camps in the district. We are proud of everything that we have accomplished and let us say, "Hoo-ray for F.D.R."

Camp L-70 at St. Joseph closed October 18, 1935, after successfully completing its assigned mission.

A—Military Bases, U.S. Army

In 1935, two CCC companies were organized for projects on the Barksdale Air Field in Bossier City. In a unique arrangement, the user agency or sponsor for these companies was the U.S. Army Air Corps.

Barksdale Field was selected for a military airfield in December 1928. A minimum of 20,000 acres was needed to locate a new airfield, and a group of citizens from Shreveport found a sprawling cotton plantation of 22,000 acres near Bossier City that was ideal for the purpose. The site was approved by the military, and construction of Barksdale Field began in 1931, when hangers, runways, and housing were built.

CCC workers assigned to Barksdale Field in 1935 were primarily responsible for building roads, developing emergency landing fields, improving drainage, and constructing targets for bombing practice.

The U.S. Army also established a CCC camp at Jeanerette. Company 2440 was assigned to develop the infrastructure of the nearby New Iberia Government Experimental Farm.

Company 3498, Camp Army-1, Barksdale Field, Shreveport—On July 5, 1935, Company 3498, Camp Army-1, was established 12 miles east of Shreveport, on the 22,000-acre Barksdale Airport Reservation, said to be the world's largest military reservation.

The first group of enrollees consisted of 80 African-Americans from the Shreveport area. Another 90 African-American enrollees came from New Orleans. The CCC workers of Camp Army-1 arrived well ahead of the camp's

Civilian Conservation Corps workers at muster, receiving instruction for the day's work activities.

commanding officer and staff, unit equipment and supplies, and trucks, and so, for a time, the men had no running water and no stoves to cook on; they had to carry water in dish pans from nearby farmhouses, and meals consisted of cold sliced meat on bread.

The campsite was overrun with weeds and grass. With no trained cadre assigned to the camp, CCC leadership picked a first sergeant from the enrollees, appointed cooks, and chose leaders who would run the physical conditioning program and set the camp in order. By early August, 16 local experienced men were added to the staff, and leadership from the user agency arrived composed of Capt. George McCoy, Jr., of the U.S. Army Air Corps, and support personnel. In October 1935, the company enrollment grew by 91 men who arrived from conditioning at Fort Benning, GA.

Work projects for Camp Army-1 were confined to improvements on the Barksdale reservation. Road building for the reservation was a major work project for the company. Camp Army-1 CCC workers built emergency landing fields and operated a portable sawmill to use timber harvested from the roads and landing fields for building bridges and making other camp improvements. The workers used a large

portion of the lumber to make targets for the field's bombing range. Camp Army-1 workers also installed telephone lines and built dams to create small lakes for recreation purposes.

In September 1935, Educational Advisor Fred A. Cummings arrived at Camp Army-1 and set up a curriculum of elementary and higher-level subjects as well as various types of vocational training. Camp Army-1 had a well-rounded religion program with a chaplain conducting services semi-monthly and local pastors supplementing the program to help meet the needs of the CCC workers. Recreational activities included different kinds of sports and an orchestra developed with instruments provided by the company.

Company 3499, Camp Army-2, Barksdale Field, Shreveport—Like Company 3498, Company 3499 was also organized in July 1935 at Barksdale Field. At midnight on July 14, 1935, 14 truckloads of company property and the commanding officer arrived to be greeted by Capt. James Monk and a cadre of 15 White enrollees of Company 1440 of Marion. The next day, 125 African-American enrollees arrived from the Baton Rouge area. Navy Ensign John B. O'Neal arrived soon after as a company staff officer. The rest of the month was spent in conditioning the men and clearing the camp site.

BELOW: *Portion of Civilian Conservation Corps Company 3598, Army-1, at Barksdale Field Reservation, Shreveport, in front of their barracks.* LEFT: *Civilian Conservation Corps crew is applying rock to a newly constructed roadbed.*

The main objective for Company 3499 was to improve the infrastructure of Barksdale Field Reservation. Projects included building 25 miles of gravel road, constructing 25 miles of dirt road with bridges, developing 2 emergency landing fields and gun ranges, planting 1,000 pecan trees along highways within the reservation, developing fire preventative roads and fire breaks, and providing drainage throughout the military base (U.S. Army 1935).

In March 1936, the work of Company 3499 at Barksdale Field ended and the company was transferred to Keithville to become Camp SCS-21. During the transfer, influenza and measles broke out among the CCC workers (U.S. Army 1937). The men went on to distinguish themselves at Camp SCS-21 by undertaking management of a vegetable gardening on a large scale. As part of Camp SCS-21's educational program, the CCC workers viewed gardening and producing vegetables and flowers to be both a good hobby and a way to have food appropriate for a healthy lifestyle.

Company 2440, Camp Army-5, Jeanerette—On June 12, 1935, an advance cadre of 16 men left Slidell Camp P-52 for Thibodaux, where they established Camp D-2, after which they went on to Jeanerette where a permanent campsite had been selected for Camp Army-5. Three miles west of Jeanerette and seven miles east of New Iberia, the site was a grove of pecans and oaks, festooned with trailing streamers of Spanish moss (U.S. Army 1935), and bounded on the north by Bayou Teche.

Other enrollees began arriving in July 1935, when Company 2440 was officially organized under Capt. W.G. Bowen as commanding officer. The New Iberia Government Experimental Farm provided the project superintendent and foremen.

Company 2440's assignment included developing the infrastructure for the Livestock Experimental Farm. On 1,125 acres of land on each side of Bayou Teche, the farm was established in 1914 to conduct experiments in livestock breeding and feeding, including developing cattle breeds that would tolerate the hot, humid climate along the Gulf coast. Ownership of the farm was transferred to the Louisiana State University Agricultural Center in 1974; the farm is now the AgCenter's Iberia Research Station.

Camp Army-5 CCC workers built 40,421 feet of fencing, 14 miles of roads, and 114,837 feet of drainage ditches and canals, and cleared 205 acres of brush that harbored a large mosquito population.

The natural beauty of Camp Army-5's setting was enhanced by shell walks, a fishing pond, and shrubbery and grass. Camp Army-5's educational and recreational programs included baseball and indoor games in the recreation hall. The camp published a newspaper entitled *The Pirogue*. Movies in nearby Jeanerette and New Iberia were favorite haunts of the camp's CCC workers in their leisure time.

LEFT: These are the Iberia Experimental Farm foremen who led the Civilian Conservation Corps work at the farm. RIGHT: Entrance sign to the State Forest supported by a Civilian Conservation Corps built stone pylon.

S—State Forest, Division of Forestry, Louisiana Department of Conservation

In 1933, when the CCC originated, the Alexander State Forest was one of the few State land holdings of significant size for a CCC camp. When State Forester V.H. Sonderegger allocated CCC camps following his visit to Washington, DC, on April 6, 1933, he proposed a CCC company for the State forest. Near Woodworth, the forest of over 6,000 acres was a prime location in many respects, with virgin pine stands, cutover areas, both bottomland and upland conditions, and wetlands resulting from springs. The forest also hosted a Division of Forestry pine tree seedling nursery that could be used for State and private camps in both training CCC workers and in production of seedlings for planting.

The assignment of a company of military veterans to the site was favorable. Most of the men served in World War I and brought with them the discipline and capability needed to make the site productive from the start. The CCC provided a means of supporting their families, and the State forest greatly benefited from the association.

Company 2429, Camp S-63, Woodworth—Company 2429 occupied a site in the Alexander State Forest about 15 miles south of Alexandria. Organized July 13, 1933, Camp S-63 was one of a few CCC companies in Louisiana made up of World War I veterans.

Initial housing was in tents, but soon huts replaced the tents. This became the only camp in the district where CCC workers were permanently housed in wooden huts. The camp's row of huts was arranged in a horseshoe shape with the kitchen, mess hall, and recreation hall located in the center of the horseshoe. Each hut accommodated four to five men and was painted red with a green roof (U.S. Army 1934).

Leche Lodge, a beautiful log building built by Camp S-63 CCC workers, was used as the headquarters by U.S. Army officers, the headquarters for using-service personnel, and, for several decades, as an administrative building for the State forest. The project superintendent was Charles F. Delaney, who, in addition to this responsibility, was the State forest nursery manager. Delaney was recognized by his peers for his excellence in working with the CCC enrollees.

Camp S-63 CCC workers were trained in various areas of vocational work, such as woodworking, forestry, farming, truck repair, and masonry. The camp hosted an excellent woodworking shop, where 19 men made signs, furniture, ax and hammer handles, and a variety of other objects for Camp S-63 and other camps in the CCC district. The CCC workers in the woodworking shop also made campsite signs carved from wood and set them in stone pylons.

Camp S-63 was a supply depot for District E. With its own trucks, the S-63 depot delivered supplies all over the State—everything from a box of tacks to a crawler tractor. For several years, Camp S-63 was the district's central vehicle repair shop, where 4 mechanics and 30 CCC workers often completely refurbished the trucks brought to them from CCC camps, turning the rebuilt vehicles out of the shop brightly painted in green with white lettering on the door panels (U.S. Army 1937).

TOP: *Leche Lodge, named in recognition of Louisiana Governor Richard W. Leche (1936-39), was constructed by Civilian Conservation Corps enrollees. It served as the headquarters site for Camp S-1 military and user agency leaders. Later it served as an administrative building for the Alexandria State Forest in Louisiana.* LEFT: *Reaching a height of 175 feet, the State Forest fire tower is the tallest in the world.* ABOVE: *Charles Delaney (left) and his brother Luther Delaney (bending over) were responsible for the State forest tree seedling nursery.*

Company 2429 was appreciated by the surrounding communities and had a significant role in developing the area. Camp S-63 CCC workers constructed 2 nurseries, 33 bridges, 100 miles of fencing with crosstie posts, 12 fish and bird ponds, 50 miles of gravel roads, 5 miles of telephone lines, 28 miles of firebreaks, and a fire lookout tower—and they planted 6 million tree seedlings.

Camp S-63 had an education program and a regimen of social activity that included a drum and bugle corps, an American Legion Post, and a Veteran's of Foreign Wars (VFW) post where 32 members of the camp signed as charter members. The camp mascot, Bill the Goat, accompanied a delegation from the camp to a VFW convention in New Orleans, where Bill made his appearance in parades.

SP—State Parks, National Park Service; Division of Wildlife, Louisiana Department of Conservation; and State Park Commission

In 1933, when the CCC was established and construction of State parks was authorized under the auspices of the National Park Service, most Southern States had no established State park system. In Louisiana, the legislature had not even authorized a State park commission under which parks might be created.

Through lenient interpretation of the Emergency Conservation Act, the Louisiana Department of Conservation met the requirements of the National Park Service (NPS) for establishing a park camp at

BELOW: A camp foreman teaches enrollees how to read blueprints for construction. RIGHT: The original Acadian home of Henry Wadsworth Longfellow is believed to be where Longfellow wrote his epic poem "Evangeline." The house was restored and then converted into a museum by the Civilian Conservation Corps.

St. Martinville. A group of citizens in St. Martinville had formed the Longfellow-Evangeline National Park Association in hope that this would help justify assignment of a park camp.

Actual development of a park commission did not happen until late 1934, but even then, the newly created State Park Commission worked without funding until 1936. After working for about a year at the Longfellow-Evangeline site and making good progress on development of the park, Company 277 was transferred and the effort at St. Martinville ended.

In 1935, the donation of a large tract of land from the Crossett Timber and Development Company and the Morehouse Police Jury provided sufficient land (over 500 acres) for a second CCC park camp—known as the Chemin-A-Haut State Park. Two other large tracts of land were later acquired and developed into State parks. Only four State parks were developed in Louisiana with assistance from the CCC.

Company 277, Camp SP-1, St. Martinville—

Company 277 was organized at Camp Dix, NJ, in May 1933. The commanding officer, Capt. I.C. Nicholas, led the company to McCall, ID, with an advance cadre of 25 CCC workers. The main body, including enrollees from New Jersey and New York, arrived in Idaho in early June and located on the shores of Payette Lake, where work involved clearing land and building roads, ranger cabins, and lookout towers. A highlight of the assignment was fighting fires in the primitive Chamberlain Basin Country, an area of Idaho so isolated that the CCC firefighters had to be flown in by plane.

In late September 1933, Company 277 and others at McCall prepared to leave Idaho for other locations. Most

of the enrollees were shipped back east, but 59 left Idaho and arrived in St. Martinville on October 20, 1933, filing off the train to find themselves slightly bewildered at the sight of a few rather curious descendants of Acadians. The Longfellow-Evangeline park area was known for its distinctive scenery and unusual historical features. Henry Wadsworth Longfellow uses this part of Louisiana as the scene for his Acadian epic poem "Evangeline," one of the best known love stories in American literature.

One of Company 277's officers described the park's "evidences of every natural beauty in the southland," noting that the "grassy woodlands, sylvan dells, sluggish bayous, sunken gardens, meadow highlands, fields of rolling green, gigantic oaks, hoary and moss covered, the pines and the magnolias and the camphor, the pecans of all varieties, the hollies and the dogwood, the ash and gum, the birds and flowers, luxurious subtropical vegetation and the alluring water course of the Bayou Teche are only a few of the innumerable natural beauties" (U.S. Army 1934).

In November 1933, a train from Fort Dix, NJ, brought 133 more CCC workers from Eastern States, and activity around the half-constructed barracks and hastily erected tents increased.

At that time, the Acadian people of St. Martinville had little communication with the world outside their community and did not fully understand how the CCC program worked. But they readily accepted the outsiders and had a great deal of hope that development of the park might help preserve part of their Acadian heritage. As well, the CCC workers developed a rapport with the townspeople through involvement in St. Martinsville social and sports events (even, in December 1933, when the CCC camp basketball team defeated the St. Martinville High School team 38 to 12. In spite of the defeat, the townspeople were impressed to learn that three of the Company 277 players had played on eastern college teams) (Humphreys 1964a).

Delays in Louisiana establishing a State park commission to work with the NPS seems to be behind Company 277's move from St. Martinville on October 27, 1934. It was not until 1936 that the CCC returned to resume work on the Longfellow-Evangeline State Park, an effort that continued for 2 years.

Today, Longfellow-Evangeline is no longer a State park, but is designated as a State Historic Site, because, although there are picnic grounds and other amenities in addition to the museum, there are no campgrounds or overnight cabins (McLaughlin 1994a). Visitors come from around the world, drawn by the history of the Acadians and Longfellow's romantic poem.

Company 478, Camp SP-4, Bastrop—Camp
SP-4 was established on a 522-acre site donated by the Crossett Lumber Company and the Morehouse Parish Police Jury, 10 miles north of Bastrop at the confluence of Bayou Chemin-A-Haut and Bayou Bartholomew. In 1762, French Canadian hunters and traders, navigating Bayou Bartholomew in the 18th century in search of pelts, are credited with naming Chemin-A-Haut Creek (Helbling 2011), a name derived from the French for "high road." Native Americans also traveled through the area in seasonal migrations.

Camp SP-4 was located on the site previously developed by Company 1491 and named Camp P-57. The work of Camp SP-57 ended in October 1935, and in November 1935, Company 478, consisting of 160 enrollees from Crawfordville, GA, under the command of Capt. T.L. Borom, arrived with the assignment of building a new State park.

CCC worker R.W. Corley described the arrival of the company in the new camp:

The change from the former site in Crawfordville was a new experience for most of the enrollees of Company 478, who were natives of Alabama and Georgia. Only a few had been west of the Mississippi River, and they all had their eyes open wide as they travelled along Louisiana roads flanked with moss-covered trees.

Despite the new sites and faces, many of the boys had a slight attack of home sickness for their native State. One thing that cheered up the youth was a big Thanksgiving dinner prepared under the careful direction of Assistant Mess Inspector, Second Lt. Bryce Alexander. The members were "just kids" again as they sat down to the appetizing meal that made their away-from-home Thanksgiving complete (U.S. Army 1937).

The CCC workers of Company 478 brought with them a background in park building. Company 478 had formed at Fort McClellan, AL, in 1933, and moved to Georgia where they worked in developing Alexander Stephens Memorial Park. When the Crossett Lumber Company donated the land for the park, no timber of commercial value was left standing, leaving a mass of pine logs and tree tops. As soon as the CCC workers became acclimated to life at Camp SP-4, they undertook the task of reconditioning the camp, and in January 1936, started a fire reduction project for the entire park, building fire breaks around the park boundaries and making topographic surveys of the area.

The 1937 Annual Report of Division E camps reported that "these experienced future builders of America have completed five cabins, laid the foundations for a new lodge building, and constructed roads and parking areas" (U.S. Army 1937).

Camp SP-4 CCC workers enjoyed the privilege of participating in various educational activities, including not only formal training in a variety of high school and vocational classes but also on-the-job training in masonry,

A portion of Company 277 was assigned in 1933 to Camp SP-1 in St. Martinville to build Longfellow-Evangeline State Park. These Civilian Conservation Corps workers came primarily from New Jersey and New York.

BELOW: *Trucks were used to move Civilian Conservation Corps workers from camp to camp and to carry them to field work sites beyond walking distance from the camp.*
LEFT: *Civilian Conservation Corps workers receiving typing instruction from a Works Projects Administration funded teacher.*

carpentry, plumbing, excavation, electrical wiring, and civil engineering. The workers received instruction at a specific time each day, and their foremen worked with them to help them see how the skills and knowledge they were acquiring could be used when the men returned to civilian life.

The Camp SP-4 CCC crews developed the park, turning the cutover wooded area north of Bastrop into a nice visitors' attraction. City and parish officials touring the area in January 1938 reported that "visitors to the park marveled at the work of the CCC workers who could build such structures without any previous training" (Helbling 2011).

Company 478's work at Chemin-A-Haut State Park ended in March 1938, and the unit was transferred to the Fontainebleau State Park at Mandeville. Local officials felt that the lack of long-range planning and appropriations from the State were contributing factors for the transfer from the site. The CCC did not return to Bastrop, but the park did receive additional assistance from the Works Projects Administration for completion of the lodge and cabins. The State allocated $3,200 to expedite this effort (McLaughlin 1994).

Company 478, Camp SP-5, Mandeville—Company 478 was transferred from work at Camp SP-4 near Bastrop to Mandeville to begin work on the Tchefuncte State Park and Conservation Reservation. Land of 5,800 acres was purchased from the Great Southern Lumber Company in late 1937. Approximately 2,700 acres of this area was later renamed Fontainebleau State Park.

Fontainebleau was first called Tchefuncte State Park because early property records of that area used its Indian name, Chifonta, which referred to a nearby river. The park's name was not officially changed until 1942. The park property originally had been part of the large Fontainebleau sugar plantation, named after the French town of Fontainebleau.

By April 1938, a village of CCC barracks and other buildings was being erected along the banks of Bayou Castaigne about a mile from Mandeville, which became the new home of Company 478, whose men developed the first phase of Fontainebleau State Park.

The park, on the north side of Lake Pontchartrain, was 50 miles from New Orleans by land and 20 miles by water. The principal portion of the land to be developed was the waterfront. The greatest challenge facing Parks Commission and CCC workers was dredging, deepening, and filling a large lagoon that would offer the area's residents a quiet spot for small boats and fishing. A master plan for the park was prepared by William W. Wells, with some modifications by the NPS, whose officials considered Fontainebleau one of the "most elaborate State parks under construction in the South, as well as one worthy of complete development" (McLaughlin 1994).

Civilian Conservation Corps workers receiving new uniforms at the time of camp establishment.

Fontainebleau's significance in the history of Louisiana's State parks system is that its development by CCC crews was not based primarily on NPS expertise. Instead, it was the first State park project constructed according to a master plan prepared entirely within the State's park organization (McLaughlin 1994).

The master plan for the park—carried out for 2 years by CCC workers and later continued by the State Parks Commission after the CCC became a casualty of war preparation—provided for two separate types of recreational development, one including public bathhouses, picnic shelters, a lodge, and vacation cottages for family use; and the other including facilities for larger groups such as Boy Scouts and fraternal and religious organizations (Humphreys 1964a).

Company 1427, Camp SP-6, Ville Platte—Chicot State Park was destined to be the last park in Louisiana for partial development by the CCC (Humphreys 1964a). The park, about 5 miles south of Ville Platte, began with 5,000 acres, and through the years grew to more than 7,000 acres.

Company 1427, consisting mostly of Louisiana enrollees, was assigned to the area in 1938, working under NPS. When the camp was established, citizens of Ville Platte acquired a 300-foot right-of-way, about 5 miles long, for a parkway from town to park entrance.

The CCC's work at Chicot had great variety. Service roads and bridges were built, but the largest effort went into a

partial clearing of a heavy growth of timber on the 2,000 acre lake bottom and constructing a mile-long levee, 4-feet high, complete with a concrete spillway (Simoneaux 1940). The State Park Commission purchased a portable sawmill and the CCC enrollees used it to convert the cleared timber into lumber for use at Chicot and other State parks.

The landscape of Chicot was as close to spectacular as possible in the Louisiana park system. The high regard for the visual beauty of Chicot's forest is understood when one reads the report by Willis King, the NPS associate wildlife technician assigned to the CCC camp (King 1939):

Chicot ... is one of the finest natural areas where the NPS has had the opportunity to develop . ...Two major forest types characterize the area. One is upland hardwoods, which clothe the low ridges . ...The climax is an oak-hickory forest, whose trees are of large size. White oak, chestnut oak, southern red oak, shell-bark hickory, bitternut hickory, hop-hornbeam, and basswood are principal members of this stand. On short slopes from the ridges to the bottomlands, American beech and evergreen magnolias are conspicuous additions to the stand. This composition gives a forest which is unusually beautiful and entirely unexpected at this southern latitude. Irregularly wooded hills rise from the water's edge, forming a long peninsula of land which provides over 40 miles of shoreline to the 2,000 acre lake. The park will be unexcelled as a wildlife refuge and for fishing.

Company 1427 remained at the park for 2 years, from 1938 through 1939. Lt. William Bartells, U.S. Navy

Reserves, was in charge most of the time. This company completed the levee, the spillway, and the large clearing and drainage project. With removal of the CCC camp, the work of completing the camp was undertaken by the State Park Commission. Proposed additional CCC companies could not be provided due to the increasing demands of national defense.

A limited amount of aid from the Works Projects Administration, however, was acquired because recreation areas were needed for developing nearby developing military camps (Polk, Livingston, Claiborne, and Beauregard) that were being built or activated after 1939.

Although the park was used as early as 1942, it was not dedicated until June 1943 (McLaughlin 1994).

D—Drainage, Bureau of Agricultural Engineering

Drainage problems are complex and the attempted solutions even more complex. The formation of independent local drainage districts have been the typical approach to dealing with such problems.

A satisfactory drainage program has the provision for proper maintenance of ditches and related structures. Due to the agricultural depression, lack of proper maintenance

resulted in ditches that were clogged with vegetation and debris. As a result, both health problems and economic losses increased (Humphreys 1964a).

The first drainage camps were authorized in 1935, and six were assigned to Louisiana. They were sponsored by the Bureau of Agricultural Engineering. This number was reduced to five and remained at this number until 1940, when drainage camps were transferred to the sponsorship of the SCS. In 1937, the five camps were located at Abbeville, Ville Platte, Thibodaux, Lafayette, and Iowa.

The CCC camps renovated many drainage channels that had fallen into poor condition during the Depression. In some places, clogged ditches stopped the flow of water, flooding farms and creating health problems. The CCC cleared and dredged the choked waterways. By 1939, the CCC drainage camps had cleared and excavated 18,400 miles of channels, built 4,300 water control structures, and relaid 250 miles of drainage tiles (Vileisis 1997). This work resulted in a significant improvement in the economy of the State.

Company 4401, Camp D-1, Abbeville—On the morning of July 19, 1935, the site for Camp D-1 was selected one-half mile west of Abbeville, LA. A cadre of 15 men from Camp Packard (F-3) in Alexandria, LA, arrived with tents and equipment to begin developing the camp. Twenty additional men arrived a few days later, and site work was under way.

On August 20, 1935, Camp D-1 was formally organized, and enrollees from Tallahassee and Tampa, FL and Macon, GA, arrived forming Company 4401. Lt. Frederick O. Rudesill assumed command of the company on September 29, 1935. Improvements in the camp were made and the morale of the CCC workers improved. Of his leadership, it was reported "under his able and dynamic leadership, and his increasing efforts to make Camp D-1 the best in the district, the men have all feel that he is an excellent commander. Working with him is not a task, but rather a pleasure" (U.S. Army 1934). Under the leadership of the commanding officer and camp superintendent, Camp D-1 was evaluated and rated excellent.

Camp life improved with building completion and grounds landscaping, and soon the CCC workers had many advantages that earlier enrollees could not boast. For recreational activities, the camp offered baseball, softball, tennis, basketball, horseshoe pitching, and various other minor indoor sports. Related to the educational program, there was a good library of books and a regular school after work hours in which elementary and high school classes were taught.

The men were trained in various fields of vocational work such as diesel engineering, dragline operation, bulldozer operation, mechanical drawing, typewriting, mechanics, and shorthand.

The parish was divided into nine drainage wards. Within these wards, drainage districts were organized. Camp D-1 had the advantage of accessing considerable mechanical equipment. On July 1, 1936, the company operated three draglines under a cooperative agreement with the Bureau

of Agricultural Engineering. They had two crawler tractors to level spoil banks and rake drainage channels of water hyacinths and alligator grass.

During 1936 alone, Company 4401 worked on 36 projects embracing a drainage area of about 400,000 acres.

Company 2441, Camp D-2, Ville Platte—On

July 5, 1935, a cadre of 25 African-American World War I veterans from Camp MP-7 at Corinth, MS, began establishing a camp at Ville Platte. A suitable and beautiful location was selected just outside of the city limits of Ville Platte, and the cadre began preparing the site for permanent buildings (U.S. Army 1935).

Under the supervision of Superintendent Leon Wall, work began on drainage projects. The first was to clear and recondition the main canals and lateral ditches of the Ville Platte Drainage District and the clearing and grubbing of Bayou Cocodrie.

Capt. Robert L. Withers arrived at the camp on July 31, and construction proceeded at a brisk pace. The first enrollees arrived on August 2, and Company 2441 was formed. Many tales are told of the hardships of those first few months—stories of the mosquito attacks and drenching rains. But, it was not long before the barren, desolate campsite had been transformed into a small village of permanent quarters for the men.

A tractor bulldozer and a dragline excavator were added to the camp equipment and immediately put to work. Several new projects were approved, namely grubbing of Bayous Nez Pique, Des Cannes, and Toulous, and reconditioning of

ABOVE: B.O. Childs was the district engineer for Louisiana's Bureau of Agricultural Engineering RIGHT: A channel being developed to facilitate drainage from agricultural fields.

LEFT: Civilian Conservation Corps workers using hand tools to improve drainage. RIGHT: Although much of the drainage was done by hand, the larger channels were cleared with the help of draglines.

the Prairie, Miller, and Mamou Gravity Drainage Districts. The CCC workers were divided into several crews and placed in different portions of the parishes of Evangeline and St. Landry.

Through a loan agreement, a log skidder was made available to pull logs and other forms of debris from main channels within water districts. By the end of 1935, a great deal of work had been accomplished, and camp equipment included three half-ton pick-up trucks, eight stake body trucks, and the tractor and excavator.

The camp became one of the show places of Evangeline Parish and the pride of District E. The company repeatedly received "Excellent" reviews from District E officers and won the Sub-District competition silver loving cup twice.

Morale of the African-American company of enrollees was excellent, and a positive relationship between the camp and the community developed. On April 4, 1937, more than 800 persons visited the camp and joined in the celebration of the fourth anniversary of the CCC. Dr. F.G. Clark, Dean of Southern University, was the principal speaker. Company 2441 was considered as a worthwhile part of Evangeline Parish. Both in work and play, the men

made a favorable impression on the residents of the parish (U.S. Army 1937).

Company 4403, Camp D-4, Lafayette— "When visitors came to Camp D-4 at Lafayette, they admired the beauty of it, the neat layout of the buildings, the shrubbery surrounding it, and the shell roads winding through it. They did not appreciate, however, the effort put into developing the camp" (U.S. Army 1937).

The campsite was originally an area called Girard Park, and it was used by the people of Lafayette for picnicking. On August 1, 1935, however, a cadre of 25 men plus 10 enrollees attached for duty arrived at the park, 1.5 miles from the city of Lafayette to form Company 4403. The site was overgrown with weeds and grass.

After a difficult period of erecting temporary tents and connecting water and electrical power from the city of Lafayette in heavy rains and summer heat, additional enrollees arrived from Tampa, FL, bringing the total to 200 men. In early September, work on the drainage projects began.

The first was at Scott, about 7 miles from camp, and consisted of sloping and leveling an old drainage ditch. It took about a week for the workers to get acquainted with

Company 2441 of Camp D-2 at Ville Platte was recognized as one of the best camps in District E, and the enrollees were respected by the local community for their efforts to improve the drainage of the area.

their fellow workers, leaders, and foremen. It, too, took that time for hands to get toughened, bodies to be able to stand the heat of the summer sun, and to learn the methods used in digging drainage ditches. The work assignment consisted mainly of draining the farm lands and swamps of three parishes: Lafayette, St. Martin, and Acadia (U.S. Army 1935).

Camp D-4 was centrally located and was an ideal meeting place for recreational activities and conferences of representatives from other camps in central and south Louisiana. Because they were near town, the workers had access to churches, schools, and movies. They also had a radio station and good athletic and educational programs. The educational advisor supervised education of those who were illiterate and provided elementary, high school, and college courses. Vocational training was provided throughout the program. Officers, technicians, and foremen from the user service taught vocational skills.

Supervisors were very interested in training the enrollees so they could find employment once they left the CCC. A well-stocked library provided a wide array of educational, fictional, and scientific reading (U.S. Army 1937).

People of the community initially had concern about a camp in their vicinity, but after a few months they realized the significance of the work being done and the excellent behavior of the enrollees. They began, then, to heap praises on the CCC workers. Obviously, the accomplishments of the camp program were well received and had a positive effect on the economy of the area

Company 4404, Camp D-5, Thibodaux—The site for Camp D-5 was a half mile north of the town of Thibodaux in Lafourche Parish. In an area of about 9 acres, the site was low, poorly drained, and overgrown when acquired by the army. On June 22, 1935, an advance cadre of 24 members from Company 1494, Springville, arrived to begin work on clearing the site. Arrival of portable buildings began on July 19, and work of unloading, assembling, and erecting buildings was performed by local civilian labor. Enrollees began arriving at the camp on August 16, and Company 4404 at Camp D-5 soon had a full complement of 200 members.

The camp was composed of the army headquarters, an office for the using service, a store room, a tool room, a dispensary, officers' quarters, engineers' quarters, a mess

Civilian Conservation Corps enrollees mustered for military inspection

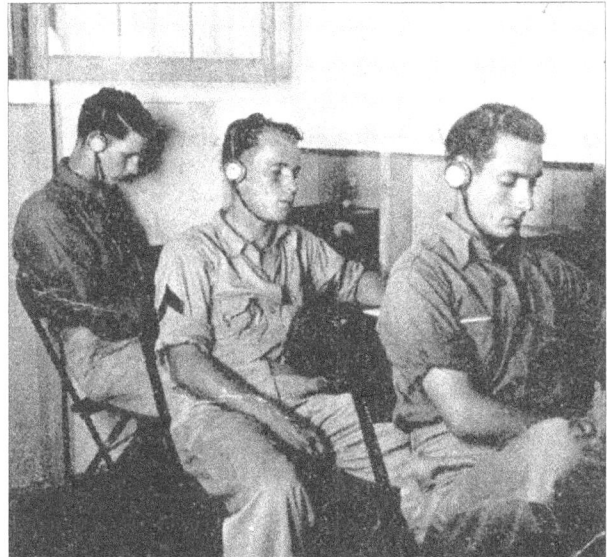

TOP: *Company 4403 men taking advantage of the camp library.*
ABOVE: *Civilian Conservation Corps workers participating in the camp's short-wave radio circuit operation.*

hall, a school, a recreational hall, a bathhouse latrine, and barracks. Water and electrical power were obtained from the town of Thibodaux.

The camp was in the sugar cane section of southeastern Louisiana. Many organized drainage districts existed, but most had not received maintenance in years, and silting caused drainage to move away from streams instead of towards them.

Restoring drainage channels presented a difficult task of clearing and excavating stumps, undergrowth, vegetation, mosquitoes, snakes, and the like. Availability of a tractor and dragline greatly facilitated work in the larger drainage channels. The flat soil surface made digging additional canals and ditches necessary. A large number of projects were needed to restore adequate drainage to the region.

One of the largest projects was a section just north of Bayou Lafourche running from Thibodaux to Raceland, about 15 miles southeast of Thibodaux. Canals were excavated that drained an area of 24,960 acres. Several thousand acres were impossible to cultivate because of poor drainage, but were returned to usable farm land. Many other projects were completed with the same positive results.

The camp acquired equipment to connect with the shortwave radio circuit maintained by the army. A well-rounded educational program was developed, and illiteracy was eliminated. The camp newspaper *Wig-Wag News* was published monthly and gained a national reputation for its excellence. Enrollee Eldridge Duplantis, of Morgan City, was the capable editor.

Company 4405, Camp D-6, Iowa—Company 4405 was one of the last African-American companies organized in District E. One mile east of the town of Iowa, on U.S. Highway 90, Camp D-6 served the area of Calcasieu and Jefferson Davis Parishes. In August 1935, Company 4405 was created with the arrival of enrollees from New Orleans and Shreveport.

Field operations began by the using service in mid-September. In 1937, the camp had an assignment of 27 projects with a total drainage area of 386,816 acres.

October 1, 1935, was regarded as an important day for the new company. It marked the formal beginning of an educational and welfare program under the direction of Education Advisor Alfred Jackson. Jackson graduated from a public school in Baton Rouge and obtained a college degree from Howard University of Washington, DC. He organized classes in elementary and high school subjects, music, letter writing, carpentry, typing, dramatics, and public speaking. However, one of his first objectives was "educating" the citizens of nearby communities where enrollees were going for out-of-camp recreation. Through appearances of various camp groups at churches and schools, by talks by the advisor, and media presentations of organized camp activities, a desirable community-camp relationship was created. "No person within the general area of Company 4405 now thinks of a CCC camp as a cross between a soup kitchen and a penal farm" (U.S. Army 1937).

One of the company's proudest leisure-time activities was the Camp Orchestra, a musical unit that was developed entirely within the organization. The orchestra provided much enjoyment and entertainment for camp personnel and became in demand both from several communities adjacent to the camp and other camps in the district. The individual to whom most credit for this achievement is due is Assistant Leader James C. Polite, the orchestra's instructor and director.

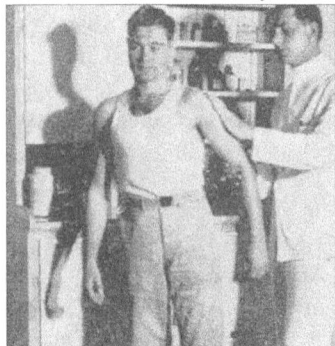

CLOCKWISE, LEFT TO RIGHT: *The camp surgeon checks the health of an enrollee. Alfred Jackson did much to educate and train Civilian Conservation Corps enrollees. Enrollees participating in a radio class—one of a number of educational subjects.*

The company published, under the sponsorship of the educational department, a monthly newspaper called *The Spade*. Under the leadership of the military officers and the user service superintendent and foremen, the CCC workers made great strides in personal development that prepared them well for work after their CCC experience.

ASCS—Agricultural Stabilization and Conservation Service

The Agricultural Stabilization and Conservation Service (ASCS) was an agency within the U.S. Department of Agriculture tasked with the implementation of farm conservation and regulation laws around the country. During reorganization of the Department of Agriculture in the 1990s, it became the Farm Service Agency (FSA). The ASCS did not become a component of the CCC program in Louisiana until 1941.

Company 6463, Camp ASCS-1. Camp Livingston—Company 6463 was not organized until May 29, 1941, and little information has been found that describes its function. It was located at Camp Livingston, a military training facility north of Pineville, LA, during World War II. Based on limited information from a few ASCS camps in other States, the CCC camp's assignment seemed to be preparing Camp Livingston for an influx of army troops. By 1941, the CCC was in decline, due primarily to the buildup of military forces.

BF—Federal Game Refuge, Bureau of Fisheries and Wildlife

In 1937, the Sabine National Wildlife Refuge was established about 8 miles south of the town of Hackberry in Cameron Parish. The large size of the refuge, 138,987 acres, made it a prime habitat for migratory waterfowl and other birds. The site consisted of brackish marshes and wetlands located between the Gulf's beach cheniers (oak ridges) and the coastal prairie and is one of the most productive marshes in North America. The Bureau of Fisheries and Wildlife (now U.S. Fish and Wildlife Service) saw an opportunity to use the CCC to develop a headquarters site on the refuge and make it more attractive to wildlife, particularly ducks and geese.

Company 1446, Camp BF-1, Hackberry—Company 1446 from Camp F-3 in Alexandria moved to a site near Hackberry in October 1938 and established Camp BF-1, only 15 miles north of the Gulf of Mexico. The campsite, Camp Sabine, had the distinction of being laid out exactly according to the district layout and specification for CCC camps. The lack of any trees made the arrangement possible. Despite the lack of trees, steady gulf breezes helped to cool the buildings.

In spite of its location, described as the "last outpost of civilization," many of the company liked the site at least as much as they liked the Camp Packard site near Alexandria where they'd come from.

The work assignment was to build up an "island" on some of the highest land on the refuge—which was only 2 feet above sea level. This elevated site was constructed to about 6 feet above sea level, and became the site on which the refuge headquarters was to be built. In addition to this

Coastal marsh typical of that of the Sabine National Wildlife Refuge. INSET: Migratory birds, such as this snow goose, find an ideal resting area in the Sabine refuge (Photograph by Eric Rueter).

project, the enrollees cleared canals and built levees to form pools, varying is size from 12 to 40 square miles each, to encourage use by waterfowl (U.S. Army 1939).

The Camp BF-1 camp enrollees did well in both educational and athletic programs. Both the softball and basketball teams were outstanding. A number of the camp's enrollees attended Hackberry High School, and school teachers instructed workers at the camp. Boat building was a vocational effort, in addition to auto mechanics, truck driving, and wood working.

SCS—Private Land, Soil Conservation Service

The first soil conservation work of the CCC was conducted under the direction of the Soil Erosion Service (SES), an agency within the U.S. Department of the Interior. The SES was established by the National Industrial Recovery Act of 1933. The first allocation of CCC camps to the SES began on April 1, 1934.

The program of the CCC personnel, under the SES, was largely restricted to gully control and terrace outlet construction. Their responsibilities included construction of ditches and check dams, clearing of streams, bank sloping and sodding, and tree planting in eroded areas (Humphreys 1964b).

The SES was absorbed by the new Soil Conservation Service (SCS) in 1935 when it was established in the U.S. Department of Agriculture. The objectives of the SCS were to determine the scientific fundamentals to improve soil conservation methods and to use these to promote conservation practices among farms, thus to maximize control of erosion on as much agricultural land as possible.

The SCS-sponsored camps worked within selected watersheds in demonstration projects on farms within designated "conservation districts." These districts were established by farmers under State guidelines and supervised by local landowners. This arrangement allowed for Federal assistance toward conservation activities without Federal control (Louisiana Department of Agriculture and Forestry 2011).

The CCC continued and expanded its work under the newly created SCS. The need for the soil conservation effort was staggering. In the mid-1930s, it was estimated that 13 million acres had lost needed protection from erosion, and that 6 million had lost 25 percent of their topsoil. Raw gaping gullies occurred between patches of stunted cotton and corn, and infertile sub-soil washed down on good bottom land (Hammett 1941).

CCC efforts under the SES and the SCS were structured as demonstration projects. A large portion of the first year's work in Louisiana revolved around a plan to return a part of the eroded, sub-marginal land to forested areas, and improve the remaining woody areas of individual farms. In the first 5 months of operation, the Minden CCC camp planted about a million trees for erosion control, mostly pine and black locust seedlings (Humphreys 1964a).

From the beginning, the CCC was a major factor in developing soil conservation programs in Louisiana. By the end of 1936, 16 camps were engaged in demonstrating erosion control methods to farmers. Later the number of camps was reduced to 11 and remained at that level until the transfer of the drainage camps of the Bureau of Agricultural Engineers to the SCS in 1940 (Humphreys 1964a).

The SCS's use of the CCC for conservation education in Louisiana was remarkable. Camps were widely distributed across the State (Natural Resources Conservation Service 2008). Most existed for only about 2 years, but each demonstrated the value of soil and water conservation to the local populace.

Education of the CCC workers was, too, an important contribution to the program. The leadership in SCS camps operated on a more flexible schedule than in more mission-oriented Forest Service camps (Humphreys 1965). Typically, time was scheduled in the workday for participation in education-related courses and studies.

Due to the nature of the camp projects, most camps were short-lived. In total, the SCS hosted about 30 camps. The following specific information about a few camps reflects the activity of most established by the SCS.

Companies 5408 and 2452, Camp SCS-1, Minden—Company 5408, located near Minden, was the first soil conservation camp in Louisiana. The site for the

camp, designated Camp Meyer after Dr. A.H. Meyer, a noted soil scientist, was originally occupied in fall of 1934 by Company 280. It was composed mostly of enrollees and military officers from New York and New Jersey who were transferred to Louisiana from Idaho. Company 280 had an uncertain existence in Louisiana, first assigned to Creston as Camp SP-2 in October 1933, then relocated several times before settling in Minden in 1934. In Minden, Company 280 began soil conservation work sponsored by the SES. In the summer of 1935, Company 280 was reassigned to the western part of the United States, and in the fall, Company 5408 replaced Company 280 at the Minden camp (U.S. Army 1937).

In 1935, the SES was merged into the Soil Conservation Service (SCS), which was placed in the U.S. Department of Agriculture, and its mission was expanded. Company 5408 was assigned responsibilities under the new sponsorship.

Members of Company 5408 were enrolled in the CCC at Tipton, GA, in August 1935, and nicknamed themselves "Georgia Crackers." Soon after being sworn into the CCC, they headed for the "Sugar Cane State" and arrived in Minden a few days later. By this time, the "Yanks" of Company 280 had departed for Utah and California.

In the fall of 1935, the company expanded with the transfer of southern Louisiana enrollees from disbanded Camp P-68 at Ansley. Addition of the Cajun French-speaking CCC workers made the "Georgia Cracker" company more cosmopolitan and resulted in some interesting interactions. Initially, some of the Georgia enrollees believed the south Louisiana Cajuns must be African-American enrollees due to their darker skin.

LEFT: *B.L. Pyburn was early State Administrator for Soil Erosion Service Camps.* ABOVE: *Farm land was completely destroyed by agricultural practices that did not limit erosion.*

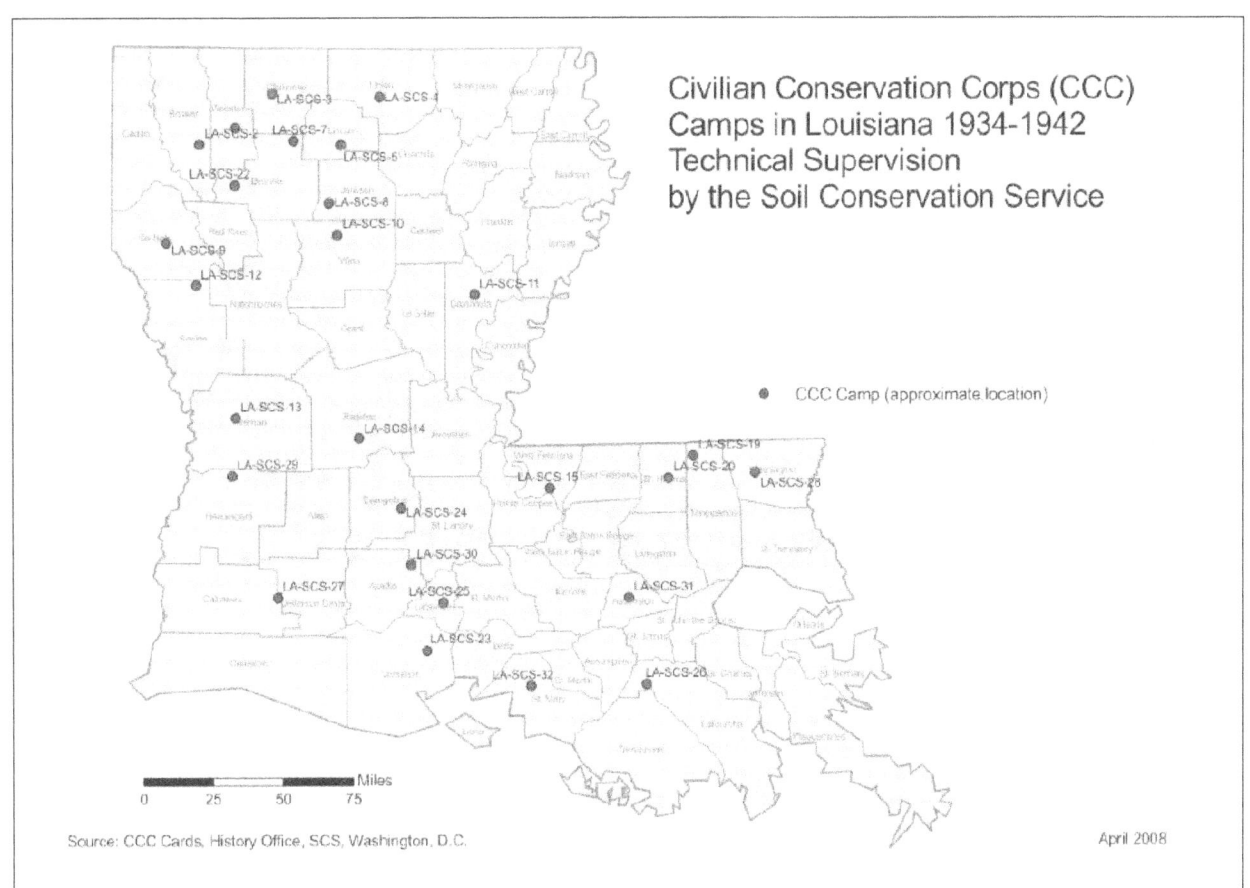

Civilian Conservation Corps (CCC)
Camps in Louisiana 1934-1942
Technical Supervision
by the Soil Conservation Service

● CCC Camp (approximate location)

Miles
0   25   50   75

Source: CCC Cards, History Office, SCS, Washington, D.C.

April 2008

Map of Louisiana showing the locations and numbers of Soil Conservation Service camps located in Louisiana from 1934 to 1942. (Natural Resources Conservation Service 2008)

In an oral interview with Anna Burns (2000), Henry Harval, a French speaking Cajun, described an interaction with his commanding officer: Asked by the commanding officer (CO) if Harval wanted a job in the officers' mess, Harval replied, "No sir." The CO asked him why not. Harval responded, "Because you like to cuss. A Frenchman don't like to make a fist!" The CO said, "Take the job and I'll help you." So Harval took the job.

"And he [the CO] helped me a lot," Harval noted. "The CO told me, 'I got a letter for you in my desk. When you leave here, get the Captain or Lieutenant to give you that letter.' I still got it—a recommendation letter."

Enrollees of Company 5408 developed an esprit de corps that saw them through a number of changes and resulted in an outstanding organization. However, on July 1, 1938, Company 5408 at SCS-1, Minden, was replaced by Company 2452 (U.S. Army 1937).

Company 2452 was composed of World War I veterans from Louisiana, Mississippi, Alabama, Florida, North Carolina, South Carolina, and Tennessee. Enrollees had a wide variety of interests, and the educational program was designed to meet the interests. Chief pursuits were in practical vocational education. In addition to the usual

woodworking and auto mechanic programs, the camp had a scientific poultry project that called for 100 chicks per week. Testing of various breeds was carried out to determine the best varieties for both food and egg production. The camp also maintained a hog husbandry project in cooperation with an enrollee who raised hogs on his own (U.S. Army 1937).

Writing and artistic ability were given expression through the publication of the camp newspaper *The Veterans' Courier*, edited by Patrick J. Rosier. It was well illustrated and given a three-star rating by publishers of the CCC national newspaper *Happy Days*.

Company 4407, Camp SCS-2, Haughton—Camp SCS-2 was established in the summer of 1935, and was located about 3 miles northwest of Haughton on the Shreveport-Minden highway (U.S. Army 1935). The enrollees were African-Americans from Louisiana and Florida.

Development of the camp went well, with buildings painted and the site landscaped. The company had a serious setback in January and February of 1936, when it suffered an influenza epidemic. At one time, there were 60 enrollees in bed and 5 of these enrollees died. Later in

51

the year, the company had an epidemic of mumps with as many as 33 enrollees bedridden at once; however, there were no deaths from the mumps epidemic.

The camp officials developed a good educational program. All enrollees participated in classes that met three times a week, and many attended three or more different classes. One show place of the camp was its vegetable garden. Camp 4407 was rated best in the sub-district eight times.

Cooperative efforts were established with farmers in the area, and demonstration projects began. In 2 years, the company performed over 40,000 workdays assisting in constructing many miles of terraces, outlet ditches, and fences. They improved hundreds of acres of pasture lands, planted thousands of acres of seedlings, and assisted farmers in planting hundreds of acres of cover crops.

All of the work contributed to the physical betterment of the farms affected, and the farmers cooperating profited financially by the contributions of the CCC enrollees. Moreover, the demonstrations installed by the CCC established soil conservation models that continue to be applied over the State and region.

Company 4409, Camp SCS-4, Farmerville—

Company 4409, known as "The Farmers" (a name resulting from the fact that the camp was located just outside the town of Farmerville) was established in June 1935. Most enrollees came from the Florida Parishes of Louisiana. The popularity of the conservation work developed steadily as demonstration projects were installed. Contracts with farmers increased as results of the CCC work were observed.

The camp had well-trained technical and supervising personnel, and the men were taught terrace construction, tractor operation, and proper use of hand tools in drainage

work. Each new job was started with instruction from the foremen in charge.

Classes were taught in soils and in the practices needed to limit erosion and improve soil productivity. Instruction was given in improved farming practices for different agricultural crops. As a result of this training, the men in a year constructed over 30,000 feet of drainage channels, dug 122 miles of furrows and ridges, sodded 33,000 square yards, and built nearly 100 miles of fencing.

The company had an outstanding safety record, both in transporting men and in carrying out their conservation work.

Company 4412, Camp SCS-7, Arcadia, and Camp SCS-22, Ringgold—On June 12, 1935, twenty-five men

from Company 1445, Camp P-69, Chatham, moved to 2½ miles south of Arcadia and began construction of Camp SCS-7. They were joined by 31 enrollees from northern Louisiana and about 120 from Florida. These groups formed Company 4412. Erosion control measures that were applied to farms under an agreement with the SCS proved their value as demonstration projects. Farmers in the camp area were attracted by the benefits that could be obtained from soil erosion practices, and soon a steady flow of cooperators signed agreements with the SCS.

By May 31, 1937, some 42,980 workdays had been spent in fields of cooperators working on erosion control demonstrations. Eighty-four cooperative agreements had been signed with a total acreage of 16,915; 246 miles of terrace lines had been established; 121 miles of terraces had been constructed; 61,135 cubic yards of soil were removed from outlet channels; 75,560 square yards of sodding was placed in outlet channels; and 150 acres of trees were planted (U.S. Army 1937).

Special interest was placed in training enrollees by members of the SCS technical staff. A recognized system of job training was established. Officials conducted classes both in the field and in the camp during morning and night hours.

The camp educational advisor from 1936 to 1940 was L.C. (Lew) Ewing. He was friendly, sincere, competent, and devoted to providing training adapted to the needs of the enrollees. Under his leadership, the camp published a newspaper, the *Rocky Crest*, which was regarded as one of the best in the national CCC program.

The experience of E.W. Carswell provides an example of the educational training that was available to the enrollees (Carswell 1985). Carswell was an enrollee from Florida and lacked 2 years from completing high school. Ewing worked with Carswell and others to obtain their high school diplomas, mostly by attending classes at the camp, and he recommended to Carswell that he should go to college. He obtained a scholarship for him to attend Louisiana Tech

University in Rustin and worked his camp schedule so he could carpool to Louisiana Tech for classes in the morning. Carswell became an educational assistant to Ewing and his experience in editing the *Rocky Crest* helped him become the editor of *Tech Talk*, the Louisiana Tech student newspaper. Carswell served in the military during World War II and returned to Louisiana Tech in a staff position. He left Louisiana Tech in 1949 and returned to Florida to enter the newspaper business (Carswell 1985). He remained thankful and proud of his experiences in the CCC that served him well throughout his life.

Carswell's educational experience was not uncommon. In 1938, Ewing scheduled 42 courses with 21 instructors for the company enrollees. Both the educational and recreational programs were excellent.

Camp SCS-7 at Arcadia closed and the company moved to Camp SCS-22 at Ringgold in April 1939. The enrollees liked the new campsite because it was nearer town and the fishing facilities at Lake Bistineau.

World War II and the Demise of the Civilian Conservation Corps

The Civilian Conservation Corps (CCC) was hugely popular and had support in Congress because of the great outpouring of public approval the CCC program enjoyed. Even U.S. President Franklin D. Roosevelt's most critical opponents agreed that the CCC was a good program that did much to provide relief to youth and their parents during the Great Depression. The program also pioneered conservation efforts across the Nation (Salmond 1967).

In 1940, however, a year of change began for the CCC. The U.S. Congress was unwilling to provide permanent status for the CCC. One reason for this attitude was that Civil Service rules for employment would have been followed in a permanent agency, and this would have eliminated a lucrative means of political patronage (McLaughlin 1994). Selection of user service supervisors for camps was frequently influenced by politicians. The salaries of these foremen were paid by the CCC. Louisiana provided a prime example of this patronage. Louisiana's governor presented names of men he wanted appointed for these positions, and State Forester V.H. Sonderegger routinely honored those requests (Cline and others 1933)—so much so that Sonderegger was found in violation of the Society of American Foresters ethical standards and was dropped from membership in his professional organization.

Another rationale for not granting permanent status to the CCC was that this would seem like a pessimistic gesture of defeat in the prolonged battle to end the Great Depression. Therefore, Congress decided merely to extend the CCC to July 1, 1943 (Salmond 1967).

In late 1939, as the world seemed headed to war, relief and public works agencies of the New Deal had to be modified to support building up U.S. military strength. In September 1940, the CCC was directed to provide enrollees with 8 hours of military basic training every week. With the surprise military strike by the Imperial Japanese Navy against the United States naval base at Pearl Harbor, Hawaii, on the morning of December 7, 1941, it became inevitable that the CCC had to be discontinued. On May 4, 1942, President Roosevelt asked Congress to appropriate funds to operate 150 camps for the next fiscal year, with the idea that the camps would contribute to national security, but Congress did not approve Roosevelt's request. The CCC was not abolished, but no operating funds were approved, and, effectively, the Nation's era of CCC work came to an end on July 30, 1942 (Salmond 1967).

Accomplishments and Influences

The accomplishments and influences of the Civilian Conservation Corps (CCC) on a national scale are so remarkable that they might seem difficult to comprehend. They were widely accepted and appreciated in all regions of the Nation. It is difficult to describe these in any meaningful way, even when limited to the State of Louisiana, without addressing these by type of impact on the State and its people.

Economic Influences

Looking back, payment of $30 for a month of hard work might seem, as some have called it, "slave labor." Putting this amount in context, however, means looking at what this wage means in the Great Depression, when more than 25 percent of the Nation's workforce was unemployed and more than 50 percent of the Nation's children and youth went to bed hungry every night.

The CCC was then a Godsend to millions of people. Over its 9 years of existence, more than 3 million men were enrolled in the organization nationally and more than 50,000 were in Louisiana (McEntee 1942). As Henry Hardtner noted, the $25 sent home to the enrollee's family enhanced the livelihood of many people and even helped save farms and other family businesses (Humphreys 1964a). Assuming that only four other family members significantly benefited from the funds sent home (this assumption is probably low since families were large at the

Such homes on worn-out farmland indicated lack of income and hope during the Great Depression.

time), more than 15 million citizens directly benefited from the CCC. Therefore, with a population of 120 million at the time, more than 10 percent of the total population was directly affected in a positive economic way. In Louisiana alone, $13 million were dispersed to dependents by enrollees (McEntee 1942).

In addition to the direct effect of the CCC workers' payments to their families, the camps themselves had a significant economic effect on the communities where they were located. Up to 24 local experienced men were employed for each camp as foremen, and the purchase of supplies, food, and other necessities had a positive effect on the local economy. Camps first thought of as threats to the community soon became seen as a highly desired economic resource.

Military Training

The U.S. Army's role was key to the success of the CCC. Military personnel organized and managed the camps, and provided the resources to make camps functional. Regular Army officers provided regional oversight that included logistics, supply, transportation, medical, and chaplain services. Reserve officers were used primarily for the management of the camps. Officers from the U.S. Navy, U.S. Coast Guard, and U.S. Marines Corps were used in the camps when numbers of army personnel were insufficient.

Reserve officers called to serve in the CCC did not receive military longevity for their service, but were considered as civilians in that regard.

The CCC program provided important training to both military personnel and CCC enrollees. The officers benefited from their opportunity to manage companies of enrollees, to obtain and provide the resources to feed, clothe, and house these men, and to arrange transportation across the country as needed. They, too, had the advantage of working with competent civilian user services specialists that enhanced their managerial experience.

The CCC's exposure to a military program provided important training to enrollees. They learned discipline, ability to work with others, and leadership skills.

The training that military officers and CCC enrollees received in the CCC program was a valuable asset when

World War II began. Training of the officers enhanced their capability to organize and manage troops, and training of the enrollees led to soldiers who had discipline and leadership skills that made for more effective military commands.

There are many reports from ranking military officers of the role of CCC trained men in the war effort. Capt. J.E. Kidd, a staff officer in the CCC program at Camp Beauregard who served with distinction as a colonel in Europe during World War II, often acknowledged the role the CCC played in the Allied victory. He stated that the CCC had prepared the men physically and mentally for the dangers and hardships imposed by war, and that their CCC job experiences enabled them to quickly qualify as specialists, key men who could be depended upon in difficult situations (Carswell 1985).

Educational Advances

Although education was not one of the initial objectives of the CCC, as camps were established it became obvious that there were opportunities to enhance the experience of enrollees. Soon education of enrollees became an important goal.

The aims of the educational program included: elimination of illiteracy, correction of deficiencies in elementary school subjects, vocational instruction, cultural and social training, character and citizenship development, and help in finding employment.

To organize educational opportunities, an educational advisor was recruited on a contract basis and assigned to each camp, with oversight from the district headquarters. Educational programs had as a focus both on-the-job training and more formalized vocational and academic experiences. The objective of the on-the-job training was to provide skills that would allow employment when the enrollees left the CCC. There was a wide range of such training—auto mechanics, wood working, cooking and baking, a multitude of construction capabilities, business, newspaper publication, and many others that would help develop responsible workers.

Advisors had to be creative in meeting educational needs. Many enrollees felt that learning welding would be an asset in finding jobs when leaving the CCC. With limited funding for educational supplies, a number of educational advisors purchased welding equipment from Sears Roebuck with the workers agreeing to pay a small

RIGHT: *Capt. J.E. Kidd was a favorite among the Civilian Conservation Corps camps because of his friendliness and leadership skills. ABOVE: Civilian Conservation Corps workers received many types of on-the-job training, learning not only construction techniques but also leadership through working together to accomplish difficult tasks, such as dam building.*

A quartet—obviously taking great pride in its dress and appearance—sings to entertain camp mates.

assessment and the advisor scraping together additional funds for its purchase. Instruction came from the user agency or the local community. A few years later, many of those trained found good jobs in various defense industries (Humphreys 1965).

The first priority in classroom training was to deal with illiteracy. Teaching enrollees to read and write was a major accomplishment. Providing elementary and high school courses that would allow them to obtain a high school diploma was another objective. When camps were near college campuses, enrollees had the opportunity to enroll in courses that would lead to a college degree.

Classroom training had a wide scope of interesting topics. Some camps provided courses in 20 or more subjects. There was considerable interest in classes in some of the social graces, such as etiquette, manners, and dancing. The advisors were pragmatic in their approach toward providing education for enrollees whose past experience ranged from virtually no education, or even illiteracy, to college training (Humphreys 1965).

Some of the most meaningful training came from the interaction of the military officers and the user agency superintendent and foreman with the enrollees. John Hunter, President of Louisiana State University, who had been an

educational advisor at a camp, noted the significant influence of these older men on the CCC workers (Humphries 1964b). They set a tone of dedication, competency, and caring that the young men aspired to follow.

Health Improvement

Each CCC camp had a medical doctor assigned to it and all enrollees were given physicals and received first aid training. Some enrollees were trained to become first-aid specialists. Dentists spent time in each camp, checking teeth and dealing with dental problems.

For most enrollees, medical care was a new experience. In general, they had previously received no medical attention, except perhaps as first-aid treatment. In addition to basic medical attention, enrollees were given information on personal hygiene and cleanliness.

In a letter of June 14, 1934, to the U.S. Department of Labor in Washington, DC, Maude Barrett, Louisiana State Director of Relief, stated that "boys who were thin, emaciated and under nourished, who had bad posture and who were slovenly, unshaven, and dirty when they came to camp, are now fine physical specimens, healthy and clean, showing a real pride in their own appearance" (Barrett 1934).

Camp sites like this one at the Valentine Lake Recreational Area became popular areas for camping, swimming, boating, and fishing.

The CCC experience resulted in a significant improvement in health of enrollees. They came to CCC camps with poor health due to poverty and nutritional deficiencies. Most gained 20 to 30 pounds in the first few months, and the combination of adequate quantities of good food and hard work improved the health of the enrollees.

Carswell (1985) talks about how proud he was of the role CCC workers played as citizen-soldiers: "Ours may not have been the best trained or the best-led army in the field, but I'm proud to tell you that our men were the cleanest ever to fight a major war. We, in the interest of personal pride and sanitation, cut our hair short and shaved our faces clean, and we washed our clothing and bathed our bodies every time we got a chance. We respected ourselves and thereby commanded respect from our home folks and our allies, as well as our enemies. I was proud of my country. I think we all were."

Carswell's comments are a testament to the influence of health-related training enrollees received in CCC camps.

Social Development

As enrollees arrived to enter camps, they were in poor condition both physically and mentally. After a few months in camp, most had a different outlook on life, showed more ambition, and were more eager to improve the conditions in which their families had been living. They learned courtesy and respectfulness. Comments like the following were common: "The boys have a new conception of the government under which they live. They have higher ideals and are broader minded. There is no doubt but that through these youths the social resources of the Nation will be conserved. This is not only the opinion of organizations which placed these young men, but the consensus of opinion of the entire Parish" (Barrett 1934).

How did the enrollees develop such an improved attitude? The interaction with others, participating in group activities such as sports, classes in etiquette and conduct taught by officers' wives, and the examples set by the officers and user services personnel began to reshape enrollee attitudes and conduct and build capability to work with and relate to others.

The Forest Service's Stuart Nursery was built and operated by CCC workers with Kistachie National Forest supervision. It produced 25 million pine seedlings annually to support the planting needs of Forest Service sponsored camps in several States.

The military experience, also, did much to build discipline and confidence. Families and friends continued to be amazed by the changes they saw in the young CCC workers. This was one of the reasons for the great appreciation of the CCC program.

Recreational Facilities

Development of recreational resources was not a major objective of the CCCs, but it did fit into the conservation emphasis of the program. Establishment of State parks and recreational sites by the Forest Service and National Park Service provided opportunities for the public to become aware of and appreciate the significant natural resources of the Nation and State, and, therefore, support for the protection of these resources.

Because of the initial lack of a State park commission in Louisiana, establishment of only four State parks were supported by the CCC. The first was the Longfellow-Evangeline State Park in St. Martinville. Work began on it under the auspices of the Department of Conservation with supervision from the National Park Service. The CCC involvement ended due to the lack of any official State park program. Once a State Park Commission was created, park development began at Bastrop (Chemin-A-Haut SP), Ville Platte (Chicot SP), and Mandeville (Fontainebleau SP).

At the Alexander State Forest, construction of recreational facilities was a priority and numerous sites were developed. At other camps, however, establishing recreational areas was not a high priority. Forest Service camps at Alexandria and Winnfield did develop significant recreational sites—at Winnfield, it was the Gum Springs Recreational Area and at Alexandria, it was the Valentine Lake Recreational Area. Both became popular sites for picnicking, swimming, camping, boating, and fishing. Other camps developed less extensive sites, most for picnicking and camping. Much of the work on such areas happened in off-season times, when the men were not working on primary responsibilities such as tree planting.

Conservation Practices

A major responsibility of the CCC program was restoring the country's depleted natural resources. Conservation tasks assigned to the camps in Louisiana included producing and planting trees, building dams to make reservoirs and fish ponds, digging diversion ditches, building levee roads, raising bridges and fire lookout towers, improving watersheds, protecting forests, developing recreational sites, and conserving soil and water resources.

Most of the camps were developed to support either forestry projects or soil and water management projects.

Tower man in a lookout using an alidade to determine the location of a wildfire. (Photograph by Elemore Morgan)

The forestry efforts were the responsibility of the Forest Service on Kisatchie National Forest lands and the Division of Forestry, Department of Conservation on private lands.

A major accomplishment was the development and operation of Kisatchie National Forest's Stuart Nursery. This nursery provided 25 million seedlings annually for reforestation activities in the Forest Service camps in Louisiana, and many in Mississippi and Texas. Tree planting was a priority on the cutover lands of National forests. During the duration of the program, over 165 million trees were planted within the State (McEntee 1942).

The forestry program of the Louisiana Division of Forestry was to improve fire protection of private forest lands within the State. This program involved establishing fire breaks, building roads to provide access to forested areas, fighting forest fires, constructing fire towers to help quickly locate and control wildfires, and erecting telephone lines to allow communication from towers to camps.

In the Forest Service and Division of Forestry camps, over 100,000 workdays were spent in fighting fires, over 4,000 miles of minor roads and firebreaks were built, and 54 lookout fire towers were erected.

The Soil Conservation Service led the effort to control soil erosion on upland soils, improve drainage of wet agricultural lands, and develop and protect watersheds. The Soil Conservation Service sponsored more camps (about 30) than any other organization, but most were short-lived—about 2 years. Their work efforts were demonstration projects on farmer-owned lands. Through these efforts, they convinced farmers of the value of soil and water conservation and management. In these camps, 35 million square yards of soil were moved in clearing and cleaning channels to control erosion and improve drainage (McEntee 1942).

In agricultural areas with extensive soil erosion, 1.5 million trees and shrubs were planted to stabilize the soil and these areas were returned to productive woodlands.

Conclusions

The Civilian Conservation Corps (CCC) was remarkable in many ways. First, the nature of the program that combined the need to put young men to work with restoring the country's depleted natural resources was unique. Second, the speed in which the program was established was astonishing. Eight days after U.S. President Franklin D. Roosevelt's March 21, 1933, message to the U.S. Congress, the establishment of the CCC was approved. On April 5, 1933, the president issued an executive order setting up the CCC. By the middle of June, camps were established and by the end of July 300,000 CCC workers were in the woods. Within 3 months from the time the president proposed the organization, the CCC program was fully operational on a national scale.

Another remarkable aspect of the program was the successful coordination on short notice among the U.S. Army and the U.S. Departments of Agriculture, the Interior, and Labor. The army had the responsibility for establishing camps, providing food, clothing, and housing for the enrollees, transporting enrollees to appropriate camps in locations across the Nation and providing for their medical and spiritual needs. The Department of Labor was responsible for establishing guidelines for recruitment and working with States to assure that quotas were met. The Agriculture and Interior Departments were charged with developing work projects and supervising the enrollees in carrying out those assignments.

Soon after the program began, it became obvious that an educational component was needed in the organization. Educational advisors were assigned to each camp and both vocational and classroom training began using all the resources that could be mustered within the camp and in the surrounding communities. Large numbers of illiterates learned to read and write, all enrollees had opportunities for academic development, many learned vocations through the training offered, and generally the CCC workers developed outstanding character and citizenship. Training in manners, etiquette, and proper conduct was provided.

Enrollees developed pride and satisfaction in cooperative endeavors, strengthened good habits of health and mental

Civilian Conservation Corps workers planted over 165 million pine seedlings on cutover forest land in Louisiana, thus beginning its restoration.

Luther Delaney (left), manager of the tree seedling nursery on Alexander State Forest, instructs Civilian Conservation Corps foremen on planting techniques for pines. (Photograph from Derwood Delaney)

development, became self-assured and confident, cultivated social skills, and developed an understanding of the economic and social world in which they lived. These were significant achievements considering the condition of the typical enrollee when arriving in camp.

Remarkable, too, was the development of the Forest Service's Stuart Nursery that provided 25 million pine seedlings annually to reestablish forests on hundreds of thousands acres of cutover forest land. The nursery was built and operated by CCC workers with supervision by Kisatchie National Forest nursery specialists and Southern Forest Experiment Station research scientists. A forest tree nursery on the Alexander State Forest also supported the CCC program by producing seedlings for planting. The CCC workers planted 165 million trees grown by the nurseries and did much to begin reforestation of the State.

Another forestry effort was to develop a fire protection system in Louisiana. Enrollees from Federal, State, and private forest camps constructed hundreds of miles of truck trails, erected fire lookout towers, and constructed forest telephone lines. The level of fire protection significantly improved as a result of the CCC efforts.

The soil conservation program carried out by the CCC camps in Louisiana resulted in substantial improvement of agricultural lands within the State. The work included terracing, gully control, strip cropping, pasture management, and planting winter cover crops for soil improvement. The enrollees constructed dikes, dams, and other water-control structures to stabilize water levels and store water. The drainage camps restored water movement in areas that tended to flood, ruin cropland, and create health problems.

The U.S. Army's role in administrating the program was significant. Enrollees were taught discipline, ability to work with others, and the basics of military leadership.

The CCC program began to compete with military preparedness movements in 1940 and the program ended in 1942. Over the 9 years of its operation, millions of lives of young men were changed for the better. They and their families were helped economically, they received valuable academic and vocational training, performed conservation tasks that began restoration of much of the Nation's natural heritage, acquired social and cultural refinements, and gained confidence and discipline. Their experience in CCC camps prepared them to become leaders in military units as World War II began and stood them in good stead as they moved into private life after the War.

In uniform voices, enrollees looked back on their experiences in CCC camps and remarked on how positively their lives were changed. Changed, too, was the environment in which they lived. They pioneered the development and large-scale application of conservation practices that continue to be applied across the State, region, and Nation.

Acknowledgments

Our appreciation goes to Matt Troll, who, as a volunteer for the Southern Forest Heritage Museum and Research Center, organized and cataloged the documents and materials in the Dr. Anna C. Burns CCC Collection; and to Jim Caldwell, of Kisatchie National Forest, who provided access to hundreds of CCC era photographs. We appreciate the work of those who made constructive comments on early drafts: John Brissette, Paul Burns, Mason Carter, and Bobby Sebastian.

Literature Cited

Barnett, J.P.; Haywood, J.D.; Pearson, H.A. 2012. Louisiana's Palustris Experiment Forest: 75 years of research that transformed the South. Gen. Tech. Rep. SRS-148. Asheville, NC: U.S. Department of Agriculture Forest Service, Southern Research Station. 64 p.

Barrett, M. 1934. Letter and attachments of June 14, 1934, to Frank W. Persons, Department of Labor, Washington, D.C. 12 p. On file with: Southern Forest Heritage Museum and Research Center, Dr. Anna C. Burns CCC Collection, Long Leaf, LA 71448.

Burns, A.C. 1968. A history of the Louisiana Forestry Commission. Monograph Series Number One. Natchitoches, LA: Northwestern State College, Louisiana Studies Institute. 137 p.

Burns, A.C. 1983. Esprit d'corps: Remembering the CCC. Forests & People. 33(1): 10-12, 14.

Burns, A.C. 1998. Oral history interview of October 17, 1998, with Joseph M. Berry. [Cassette tape]. Long Leaf, LA: Southern Forest Heritage Museum and Research Center, Dr. Anna C. Burns CCC Collection.

Burns, A.C. 2000a. Oral history interview of September 13, 2000, with Otis and Ethyl Miller. 16 p. Unpublished document. On file with: Southern Forest Heritage Museum and Research Center, Dr. Anna C. Burns CCC Collection, Long Leaf, LA 71448.

Burns, A.C. 2000b. Oral history interview of September 20, 2000, with Daniel Guidry, Harold Webre, and Henry Huval. 8 p. Unpublished document. On file with: Southern Forest Heritage Museum and Research Center, Dr. Anna C. Burns CCC Collection, Long Leaf, LA 71448.

Burns, E.B.; Burns, A.C. 1997. Oral history interview of May 27, 1997, with Dr. M.J. Hair. [Cassette tape]. Long Leaf, LA: Southern Forest Heritage Museum and Research Center, Dr. Anna C. Burns CCC Collection.

Carswell, E.W. 1985. Comments for delivery at the 50th anniversary reunion of Company 4412 at Arcadia, LA, June 1, 1985. 20 p. Unpublished document. On file with: Southern Forest Heritage Museum and Research Center, Dr. Anna Burns CCC Collection, Long Leaf, LA 71448.

Cline, A.C.; Ayres, P.W.; Chapman, H.H.; Reynolds, H.A. 1933. Political activities in the Civilian Conservation Corps: Committee report to New England Section, Society of American Foresters. Journal of Forestry. 31: 914-919.

Daniels, R. 1971. The Bonus March: An episode of the Great Depression. Westport, CT: Greenwood Publishing. 370 p.

Gilbert, C.J. 1941. A study of the leisure-time training of five selected youth-serving agencies. Baton Rouge, LA: Louisiana State University, School of health and physical education. 89 p. M.S. thesis.

Hammett, J.W. 1941. Progress in soil conservation in Louisiana. Louisiana Conservation Review. 10: 22.

Harper, A.C. 1992. The Civilian Conservation Corps and Mississippi: A New Deal success story. Hattiesburg, MS: University of Southern Mississippi, Graduate School. 91 p. M.S. thesis.

Helbling, W. 2011. Camp Morehouse recalled: CCC men built Chemin-A-Haut north of Bastrop. www.bastropenterprise.com/features/x1405310206/Camp-Morehouse-recalled. [Date accessed: June 10, 2011].

Helms, D. 1965. The Civilian Conservation Corps: Demonstrating the value of soil conservation. Journal of Soil and Water Conservation. 40: 184-188.

Humphreys, H.D. 1964a. In a sense experimental: the Civilian Conservation Corps in Louisiana. Baton Rouge, LA: Louisiana State University, Department of History. 195 p. M.S. thesis.

Humphreys, H. 1964b. In a sense experimental: the Civilian Conservation Corps in Louisiana, part 1, origin and nature of the experiment and its role in conservation. Louisiana History. 5: 345-367.

Humphreys, H. 1965. In a sense experimental: the Civilian Conservation Corps in Louisiana, part 2, conservation of human resources. Louisiana History. 6: 27-52.

King, W. 1939. Report of National Park Service on Chicot State Park. Memorandum of May 31, 1939, to the Regional Director, National Park Service. Long Leaf, LA: Southern Forest Heritage Museum and Research Center, Dr. Anna Burns CCC Collection. 3 p.

Louisiana CCC Oral History Project. 2011. http://www.angelfire.com/clone2/timphilips/history.html. [Date accessed: May 21, 2011].

Louisiana Department of Agriculture and Forestry. 2011. History of the Louisiana conservation program. http://www.ldaf.state.la.us/portal/Portals/0/SWC/ConservationCommittee/2008-03-04_16_34_40--Microsoft_Word_-_History_of_the_Louisiana_Conservation_Program.doc.pdf. [Date accessed: July 7, 2011].

McEntee, J.J. 1942. A brief summary of certain phases of the CCC program, Louisiana, period April 1, 1933-June 30, 1942. Washington, DC: Federal Security Agency, Civilian Conservation Corps. [Not paged].

McLaughlin, S.E. 1994. The role of the Civilian Conservation Corps in the founding of Louisiana's State parks system. Baton Rouge, LA: Louisiana State University, School of Landscape Architecture. 112 p. M.S. thesis.

Natural Resources Conservation Service. 2008. Civilian Conservation Corps (CCC) Camps in Louisiana 1934-1942. www.la.nrcs.usda.gov/partnerships/Map_CCC_Camps_LA.pdf. [Date accessed: June 15, 2011].

Oxley, H.W. 1936. CCC camp leisure-time programs. School Life. 21: 258-259.

Salmond, J.A. 1967. The Civilian Conservation Corps: A new deal case study. Durham, NC: Duke University Press. 240 p.

Simoneaux, N.B. 1940. Chicot State Park. Louisiana Conservation Review. 9(2): 29-32.

Sonderegger, V.H. 1934. The Civilian Conservation Corps. Louisiana Conservation Review. 4: 49-51, 55.

Troll, M.; Burns, A.; Barnett, J. 2010. Louisiana boys of the CCC. Forests & People. 60(1): 10-11, 13.

U.S. Army. 1934. Memories of District E, Civilian Conservation Corps Fourth Corps Area, 1934. Little Rock, AR: Parke-Harper Company. 110 p.

U.S. Army. 1935. Official annual for District E, Civilian Conservation Corps, Fourth Corps Area, 1935. Baton Rouge, LA: Ramires Jones Printing Co. 231 p.

U.S. Army. 1937. Official annual for District E, Civilian Conservation Corps, Fourth Corps Area, 1937. Baton Rouge, LA: Direct Advertising Company. 243 p.

U.S. Army. 1939. Official annual for District E, Civilian Conservation Corps, Fourth Corps Area, 1939. Baton Rouge, LA: Direct Advertising Company. 230 p.

Vileisis, A. 1997. Discovering the unknown landscape: A history of America's wetlands. Washington, DC: Island Press. 433 p.

Wakeley, P.C. 1935. Artificial reforestation in the southern pine region. Tech. Bull. 492. Washington, DC: U.S. Department of Agriculture, Forest Service. 115 p.

Wakeley, P.C. 1954. Planting the southern pines. Agricultural Monograph 18. Washington, DC: U.S. Department of Agriculture, Forest Service. 233 p.

Wakeley, P.C.; Barnett, J.P. 2011. Early forestry research in the South: a personal history. Gen. Tech. Rep. SRS-137. Asheville, NC: U.S. Department of Agriculture Forest Service, Southern Research Station. 90 p.

Wandall, L.C. 1935. A Negro in the CCC. The Crisis. 42: 244, 253-254.

Willis, J.M. 2001. Civilian Conservation Camp #1495, Nickel Springs, Louisiana. 10 p. Unpublished document. On file with: Southern Forest Heritage Museum and Research Center, Dr. Anna C. Burns CCC Collection. Long Leaf, LA 71448.

Wimbush, S.M. 1972. Louisiana: The Civilian Conservation Corps in District E, 1933-1942. Baton Rouge, LA: Louisiana State University, Department of History. 88 p. M.S. thesis.